How to be a Successful Expert Witness

Book 4 in the 'Creating a Successful LNC Practice' Series

Patricia W. Iyer, MSN RN LNCC

The Pat Iyer Group
Fort Myers, FL

Copyright

How to be a Successful Expert Witness

Cover design and layout by Douglas Williams

Editorial support by Constance Barrett

Published by:

The Pat Iyer Group
11205 Sparkleberry Drive
Fort Myers, FL 33913

Disclaimer

with the understanding that the Publisher is not engaged in rendering legal, accounting or other professional services. Neither the Publisher nor the Author shall be liable for damages arising herefrom.

The fact that an organization or website is referred to in this work as a citation or a potential source of further information does not mean that Author or Publisher endorse the information the organization or website may provide or recommendations it may make.

Further, readers should be aware that internet websites and email addresses listed in this work may have changed or disappeared between the time this work was written and when it is read.

This product contains affiliate links for products that Pat Iyer recommends for legal nurse consultants. She may receive compensation for her recommendations.

This product is for sale. To purchase a copy, and to collect your valuable free reports, go to: **www.legalnursebusiness. com.**

ISBN-13: 978-1530682140

About the Author

Patricia W. Iyer, MSN RN LNCC

President, The Pat Iyer Group,
Fort Myers, FL

www.legalnursebusiness.com

Patricia helps legal nurse consultants get more cases, make more money and avoid expensive mistakes through her coaching program, www.LNCAcademyinc.com. From 1989 to 2015, she was the President of Med League Support Services, Inc, which provides legal nurse consulting services to personal injury, malpractice, and product liability attorneys. She is a prolific author who has written, edited or coauthored over 800 articles, chapters, case studies, webinars, and online courses on a wide variety of nursing topics.

In the fall of 2008, Ms. Iyer launched a series of teleseminars for LNCs, now available on the www.legalnursebusiness.com website. Ms. Iyer is a well known and respected legal nurse consultant. She served for five years on the Board of Directors of the American Association of Legal Nurse Consultants, including a term as president. She was the chief editor of the Legal Nurse Consulting: Principles and Practices, Second Edition, the core curriculum for legal nurse consulting and Business Principles for Legal Nurse Consultants. She also served as the chief editor of the AALNC's online course. Ms. Iyer is certified as a legal nurse consultant by the American Association of Legal Nurse Consultants. AALNC awarded her with the Lifetime Achievement/Distinguished Service Award and with the Volunteer of the Year Award.

Reach Pat at **patiyer@legalnursebusiness.com**

Client Testimonials

"I have been a Legal Nurse for a while, and I have been doing a pretty good job at marketing, but I felt lost because I am a nurse. Since attending the webinars, it has enhanced my confidence and marketing knowledge."

RITA BUETTNER

"Pat has been a tremendous help to me in my career as a legal nurse consultant and life care planner. I thank her for publishing her expertise and work samples. When I had ideas I wanted/needed to demonstrate in a report, I would go to her reference books and find just the approach I wanted to take."

LESSIE CHAPMAN

"For many years, I have had the incredible opportunity to subcontract for Pat Iyer, MSN, RN, LNCC in her previous business, Med League Support Services. I learned a great deal and know that the quality of my work has improved under her and her staff's guidance. I learned Pat Iyer's unique method of organizing and tabbing records which is helpful not only initially working with case records but during testimony as an expert witness. I definitely improved my writing skills, learned better ways of expressing my opinion, and decreased the use of the passive voice in my reports. I also learned how to sharpen my technique in critiquing an opposing life care plan."

LINDA HUSTED

"Pat is always informative, I always learn something new and valuable."

Toni McKee

"I've watched several of your YouTube videos and I have gained insight about the legal nurse consulting practice. I think your accomplishments are amazing and you are definitely a role model that I plan to follow. You have not only made an impact on count- less lives you have also positively influenced nursing in such a unique way. Thank you again."

Shanea Milton

"AANLCP recently had the pleasure of hosting an educational webinar with speaker, Pat Iyer. The topic was on legal writing. Pat was most professional in her presentation. She was well prepared, knowledgeable about the subject matter, AND attentive to time and open to questions. The feedback we received from our attendees was very positive with comments such as:

- *'This presentation was the best one of our whole series thus far!'*

- *'I was furiously taking notes. She has so much to share.'*

- *'I thought I was a pretty good writer, but after this great presentation I found I have a lot to learn.'*

AANLCP would welcome Pat Iyer back as a speaker at any time. She is the consummate professional."

Victoria Powell, President of American Association of Nurse Life Care Planners

"Pat's mentorship has been essential to the growth and success of my business. She stresses the importance of marketing and guides me every step of the way. When I have cases from attorneys, Pat gives me expert input so that I have confidence that my finished product is of high quality. The positive responses and repeat business make this program invaluable to me."

ILENE SCHWARTZ

"Great advice as ALWAYS. Pat never lets us down. There are few, if any, people in this business that are willing to provide advice for free. Pat truly wants us all to succeed just as she has for all these many years. Thanks Pat!"

SHERRI STEWART

"Please send me information about any of your webinars. They are awesome."

WENDY VOTROUBEK

"I was overwhelmed with so much I realized that needed to be done. With Pat's help and the discussions with the other nurses about subcontracting on our LNC Academy Inc Q&A call, I learned so much that will help my business grow. I learned how to improve my case analysis and report writing. And this is only the tip of the iceberg."

DEBBIE WUERL

Introduction

You say to yourself, "I can't believe I am raising my right hand to tell the truth, so help me God." Being an expert witness is a challenging and rewarding role.

This book is designed for expert witnesses who want to improve their skills, get more cases, and feel more confident when performing. It will help you strengthen your skills in this demanding field.

In 1987, I got a phone call that changed my life. A defense attorney asked me to review a case as an expert witness. This was my first case. Shortly afterwards, I got a call from a second defense attorney who casually mentioned that trial for the second case was set for 2 months later. Much to my shock, I was in the courtroom testifying as an expert only 2 months after I started my career. I testified as a medical surgical expert for 20 years. Additionally, at the same time I summarized medical records of seriously injured plaintiffs and testified as an expert in medical records under the Federal Rules of Evidence 1006. All told, this amounts to almost 30 years of experience as an expert.

This book draws on my experiences both as an expert witness and one who has trained hundreds of experts - nurses, physicians, and a variety of healthcare professionals. There is a lot at stake in medical malpractice cases. You want to do your best. By buying this book, you have made a great investment in increasing your knowledge.

Use this book to read through, refer to, and consult to gain a greater understanding of the role of the expert witness. I urge you to approach being an expert on a case as a tremendous opportunity and a huge responsibility. Engage in your work with professionalism and commitment. The attorney and his client are counting on you.

The information in this book is applicable to any type of healthcare expert witness, although my frame of reference is often nursing experts. If you are not a nurse, take the tips I share and apply them to your expert witness role.

The book you are holding is the fourth book in a series I began in 2016, named **Creating a Successful LNC Practice**. It is my intention to share the knowledge in this series that will help you grow your business.

Book 1 in the **Creating a Successful LNC Practice Series** is called *How to Start a Legal Nurse Consulting Business*. It takes you from the point when you leave your LNC training program and enter the world of becoming a business owner. You will learn how to develop the mindset and attitudes that allow entrepreneurs to thrive. I cover how to set up and manage your business, track your finances, get your first case and create a professional image that attracts clients to you. I give you tips on how to reach out to attorneys and work your network. This book is ideal for both the new and more experienced LNC business owner.

Book 2 in the **Creating a Successful LNC Practice Series** is called *Legal Nurse Consultant Marketing*. This is a comprehensive compilation of tips, techniques and technology. You will explore how to develop your marketing plan and website, and to share your expertise to attract attorneys to you. Presenting at attorney conferences or law firms involves skills you will learn in this book. You will find out how to harness the power of video by creating videos that highlight your skills. Unsure about how to close the deal? The chapter on sales walks you through the process of bringing the case in. You will discover techniques to become more persuasive in your marketing. Take advantage of the two chapters on exhibiting to crack the code on one of the most successful ways to meeting attorneys to build a customer base. I wrapped the book up with a chapter that answers common marketing questions. This book has something for LNCs with all levels of experience, from new to experienced.

Book 3 in the **Creating a Successful LNC Practice Series** is called *How to Analyze Medical Records: A Primer for Legal Nurse Consultants.* Use it to get tips and techniques for organizing paper and electronic medical records, the backbone of our business. You will gain an understanding of how to screen a medical malpractice case for merit and discover clues for detecting tampering with medical records. The book covers the pros and cons of electronic medical records, including how they introduce risk into the documentation of patient care. Two final chapters focus on how to polish your work product to create your strongest professional appearance. You will gain critical insights on how to strengthen your ability to analyze medical records - to gain more clients and earn more money.

Invest in these books at **www.legalnursebusiness.com**. Send me your comments and suggestions at patiyer@legalnurse-business.com.

I work with LNCs who want to get more clients, make more money and avoid expensive mistakes. When you are ready to make a financial and emotional commitment to growing your business, check out LNCAcademyinc.com. Let's work together to make your dreams come true.

Contents

Getting Cases and Polishing Your Resume or Curriculum Vitae

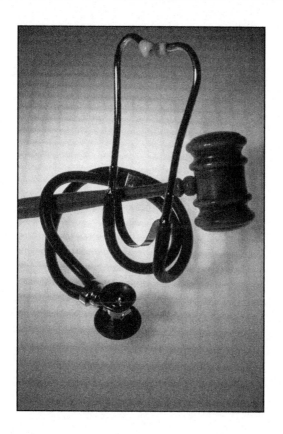

Getting Cases and Polishing Your Resume or Curriculum Vitae

Does this sound like you?

You have never reviewed a case as an expert witness before but you would like to try this intriguing role.

You have reviewed cases as an expert and would like to do more cases.

You receive a call from a legal nurse consultant who asks if you would be willing to review a case for her client.

You meet an attorney who asks if you review cases as an expert witness.

You have a friend who is an expert witness who tells you that you would be great at this kind of work.

Cases could come to you by any of these routes. Getting your first case could be the hardest or easiest thing you have done.

Your clinical knowledge is the primary reason why you are attractive to an attorney as an expert witness. The nurses who are in highest demand work in medical surgical, labor and delivery, and long term care settings, in my experience as an LNC who supplied experts to attorneys for over 25 years. However, virtually any type of nurse could get sued. At the end of this chapter, I included a list of over 90 types of nursing specialties which may require the services of a nursing expert witness. Physicians experts in most demand are orthopaedists, obstetricians, and internists.

Who Finds You?

There are a number of ways you can demonstrate your expertise in your clinical area and come to the attention of a person looking for an expert. Some attorneys do their own searches; some ask a paralegal (usually an employee) or expert witness broker to supply resumes of experts or offer recommendations. A broker could be one of several types of people - healthcare professionals such as doctors, nurses, physicians assistants, or laypeople.

When the attorney hires a broker to locate an expert to review a case, in one model, the attorney pays a flat fee to the broker to supply an expert witness. The broker puts the expert and attorney together and then is typically not involved in billing for the services of the expert after that point. In another model, the broker collects a fee based on an hourly rate for the expert's services, pays you a set fee and keeps a portion of the fee to cover the broker's overhead. In this arrangement, you are a subcontractor to the broker and will receive a 1099 if you earn $600 or more in a year from the work done on the case for the broker.

Visibility

You might come to the attorney or broker's attention in one of several ways. First, you might give a presentation at a nursing or medical conference. Healthcare associations list their upcoming events on their websites with an agenda and speaker bios. You might be referred by a colleague who is an expert witness in a different clinical area or has the same clinical background as you do but has a conflict of interest with the case. One of your colleagues who is an expert witness may decide you would be great at it and raises the subject of being an expert.

Attorneys talk to each other, participate in list servs and ask for word of mouth referrals to experts. An attorney may hire you to review a case after seeing you perform on another case. The opposing counsel taking your deposition could turn into a client in the future.

I have a vivid memory of a contentious plaintiff attorney who was angry with my deposition answers as an expert for the defense. After the case settled months later, he called me to review a case for him. "I like the way you stood up to me", he explained.

New Experts Can Get Cases
Is never having been an expert a deterrent to being hired? Some people who hire expert witnesses are reluctant to take a chance on a person who has never reviewed a case before. Years ago an attorney told me, "I don't want to hire you if you have never testified." "If no one gives me a chance, I will never get to testify", I replied. He did not hire me, but another attorney was willing to give me my first case. On the other

hand, some attorneys prefer to hire new experts, believing that they have greater credibility with a jury than a very experienced expert.

Publications – in Journals or Online

Your publications in clinical journals may bring you to the attention of those seeking experts. Your credibility is increased by having publications in scholarly journals or on scholarly websites, particularly those of your professional specialty.

In my experience, expert witnesses used to be attacked for having websites and listings on online directories of experts. I believe that stigma is fading as it becomes so common for attorneys to have websites for their practices. Blogging is a great way to demonstrate your expertise and may be the way you are found.

Be exquisitely aware that anything you put into a publication or on your website can and will be reviewed by the opposing counsel. Be prepared to be confronted with something you have written that might contradict your opinions about a case. You should think this through at the time you are preparing a report or testifying.

Pros and Cons for Working as a Subcontractor

You may get a call to review a case from an expert witness location broker. The advantage of working for a broker is that the case comes to you through the marketing efforts of the broker. In effect, the inquiry about the case lands in your lap without the need for you to market to get the case. It can feel like "found money" to get a call out of the blue asking you if you want to review the case.

The broker may provide added value with services such as organizing the medical records, proofing your report, communicating with the attorney for you, and handling the billing and collection procedures. Busy clinical experts often appreciate this assistance. Working through a broker provides you with someone you can call for support, training or advice. The attorney who is pleased with your services may return to the broker with additional cases for you to review.

The cons of working with a broker relate to the billing arrangement. The model in which the broker takes a portion of the hourly rate may result in you receiving less per hour than if you billed on your own, depending on your billing rate. Very experienced and busy experts might not be willing to accept a lower hourly rate than their typical rate. On the other hand, some are happy to turn over the billing and collections activities, and to get a case without marketing, and therefore are content with being a subcontractor for some or all of their cases.

Your agreement with the broker may preclude you from working directly with the attorney for additional cases. The expert witness world is a small one; an expert who violates the agreement will most likely be found out.

Are You an Expert?

It is essential to consider the nature of the case (either or your first or any subsequent case) before you agree to accept it.

- Are you truly experienced and expert at the type of case?

- Were you working in the clinical area at the time of the case?

- Do you have a depth of knowledge about the clinical issues involved in the case?

- Are you comfortable in stating you are familiar with the standard of care at stake in the case?

No one is helped by you taking a case when you cannot say "yes" to *all* of these questions. Your credibility is rooted in your "yeses". It is an ethical and honorable decision to be honest about your background and decline a case which does not match your background. The attorney appreciates this response and often keeps you in mind for future cases that are right for you.

Getting More Cases

The best way to get additional cases as an expert is to have these characteristics:

- Be easy to work with. There is no room for prima donnas in this role.

- Be nice to support staff, attorneys, brokers, opposing counsel, judges and juries.

- Promptly return calls and adhere to deadlines.

- Maintain a clinical role in some fashion. It is vital to your credibility to have hands on experience with patient care.

- Continually ask for feedback on how you did – your report, your testimony, your analysis. Look for ways to improve.

- Be honest and ethical.

Your Resume or Curriculum Vitae

The bulk of this chapter shares tips you can use to hone your resume or CV to make the best possible presentation of your skills. Your primary purposes are to convey your expertise, tell who you are, and show your accomplishments. Your expert witness career will be stopped in its tracks if your first impression is inadequate. I know when I reviewed experts' credentials as a broker, I rejected many expert witness candidates just based on what I saw on their resume or CV.

Experts present their credentials to an attorney or broker in the form of a resume or curriculum vitae (CV). What's the difference? A resume is a concise one- to two-page document that highlights your skills, education, and experience. A CV is a longer document prepared by people with extensive teaching, research, or publishing experience.

The difference between a resume and a CV is primarily in the area of focus and length. A resume briefly describes your primary areas of responsibility. A CV provides a greater depth of information. Both documents include strong action words to emphasize accomplishments like "created", "initiated", "saved", "accelerated", "launched", "strengthened", and "broadened". For example, a healthcare manager might state he saved the hospital $100,00 by changing to a less expensive piece of equipment or he launched an initiative to decrease the number of patients who left without treatment from the emergency department.

A CV has no set number of pages. It can be three pages or longer. Many experts list every publication and accomplishment.

Your resume or CV is your first opportunity to make an impression on your prospect, client, or potential employer. It is an important document for you to market your skills as a legal nurse consultant or expert witness. People will use it to determine if they want to give you a chance.

I have looked at thousands of resumes and CVs. The documents I saw came from people who wanted me to hire them as an employee or as a subcontractor. I can tell at a glance if the individual knows how to coherently put together his or her credentials.

Documents with typos automatically went into my reject pile. If people cannot proofread their own resumes and CVs, I know they are not going to be able to proofread the kinds of involved reports prepared by experts.

It is best to have only one version of a resume or CV that describes your professional accomplishments and contributions. When you're a testifying expert, it's not very comfortable to be up on the stand and have a second or third version of your CV appear in court that isn't the one you've supplied to the attorneys. You don't ever want to give the impression that you're trying to hide something.

Formatting

The heading of your document is the place to provide your vital contact information. I have seen occurrences when the expert accidentally left off details such as telephone number, mailing address, and email addresses. I have found errors in these details, which make it very difficult to reach the person. Have a complete and accurate heading on the top of the first page of your document.

Use an appropriate and professional email address. It is easy and free to set up a Gmail address. Avoid inappropriate email addresses like **hotmomma@hotmail.com, greatdoc@yahoo.com**, or **poodlelover@gmail.com**.

Next, list your education and your certifications. A listing of education typically starts with your highest academic degree and then works backwards. Include any certifications you hold, specifying the type of certification and the year it was awarded. Spell out the name of the certification because not everyone is familiar with the abbreviations.

Provide your work experience. It is not necessary to list the street address and phone number of your employers. What is important is to identify where you worked, your job title at the time, and your major responsibilities and accomplishments. It's more impressive to write down that you were a manager of a department that served over 30,000 patients per year and that you trained and supervised 40 RNs than it is to say that you were the nurse manager of an emergency department. Physicians should list the facilities where they have privileges.

Avoid having dull job descriptions. Legal nurse consultants who are marketing to attorneys may be asked for a resume and should be emphasize their clinical knowledge and publications. This helps to demonstrate a breadth of knowledge or a deep area of expertise in a particular clinical area.

Professional association memberships are credentials that are commonly stated in addition to the accomplishments I have mentioned. Include any leadership positions you assumed within these organizations.

Curriculum Vitae

The content of a CV expands upon the education, certifications and employment of the individual. This person may have been involved in research, teaching, grants, and other activities. If you are a professor, list your area of clinical involvement. A professor who contacted my legal nurse consulting firm about doing expert witness work did not specify the clinical areas where she supervised students. That makes a difference in terms of what kinds of cases my company could forward to her.

You may see grants and awards listed in the curriculum vitae. Sometimes you'll see academic activities of that person if he or she is in a faculty position.

Publications

List publications on your CV. Gaining credibility through writing is an impressive way to boost your legal nurse consulting career. Publications in respected peer-reviewed journals carry more weight than those in non-peer-reviewed journals. If you have contributed to a book that has not yet been published, list the publication date as "in press". Enhance your career as an expert by seeking opportunities to become published. Get more guidance on how to do this by reading Patricia Iyer and Al S. Brown, *How to Get Published*, available at **www. legalnursebusiness.com**.

Continuing Education Programs

Occasionally, I see resumes that list continuing education programs. Sometimes it is not clear if these are programs the expert attended or taught. It looks like you are trying to bulk up your credentials if you list continuing education programs you attended. It is assumed you would keep up in your field. Listing programs you taught can be problematic because it makes it easy for opposing counsel to ask you to produce the course materials that would relate to your opinions as an expert witness. The attorney hopes to see information in your materials that contradicts your opinions in the case. I don't see the point of making the job of opposing counsel easier.

Design Principles

The design of your resume or CV will attract or repel your reader. It is that simple and critical. Your document must be easy to read and follow and be succinct. By succinct, I mean you do not need to list every single professional thing that you've ever done in your life. List those that will show your qualifications for the role of expert witness.

Fonts

Use a size 12 font. Don't use a smaller font in order to adhere to a restriction to keep your resume to two pages. This rule is not as important within the legal world. I looked at a two-page resume that came to me from an individual who was interested in doing expert witness work for my LNC business. She used a size 9 font. I know she wanted to keep her document to two pages, but she ended up submitting a document that was difficult to read.

Think about the readability of the font you choose. Select one font; keep it clean and simple. Use standard fonts such as Times New Roman, Georgia, and Calibri. Avoid very artistic fonts – the ones that are written out in script, almost like handwriting. It's going to be difficult for your viewer to read those.

Use bold sparingly. Use it to amplify parts of your document such as the name of the facility where you worked or your job title. Avoid italics because they are hard to read. Don't use bold and underline together because that's redundant. Before we had computers, the only way we could emphasize documents was by underlining them. Putting underlining under bold is a carryover from the typewriter days.

Margins

One-inch margins are ideal. Some people try to stretch the document by having one-and-a-half-inch margins, which looks like padding. Some people make narrow margins so that they don't have longer documents; then the page looks crowded. It's better to use an extra page than it is to have a really narrow margin.

Page Numbering

Page numbering is important. Your document could be dropped, and the pages could get out of order. Help your reader by putting your name and page number on every page. (The page number does not go on the first page.)

I can spot people who don't know how to use the automatic page numbering. They type in their name and the page number at the top of each document. When I open up the document and check it or fix spacing for that individual before returning it to them, their header jumps down so that it's at the bottom of the page instead of at the top of the page. Learn how to use the automatic page numbering of your software. That will separate you from the amateurs.

Bullets

You may use bullets when you have a lot of short phrases. We have been trained by looking at the internet to do a lot of scanning as opposed to reading, so we appreciate bullets.

Style

Make sure that you describe your past job experience in past tense and your current job in present tense. Start with your most current education, job or business, publications, if you have them, and then work backwards.

Spell out abbreviations. Remember that most attorneys are not familiar with medical terms, abbreviations, and other aspects of medical language. Don't use *nurse speak* – when we drop off words in a sentence and write like we are charting on a medical record. Write in full sentences so that the reader doesn't have to fill in information.

Use *parallelism*, which refers to selecting consistent forms of a word. For example, you might write that your job involved, "identifying patients who needed assessment, creating plans of care, and providing nursing care". Use the same form of that verb throughout that sentence. That's also a good point to remember when you're writing reports.

Logically name your file when you save it. Don't name it as "My CV 2016". Name it with your name, your first name, your last name and then CV (PatriciaIyerCV). Keep in mind that if you're emailing your CV or resume to an individual, the recipient will want to save your file with a name that makes sense.

Look at your document to make sure that it's complete. Make sure that you've included your contact information – name, address, phone number, and email address. Double check all details to make sure they are correct.

Exclusions

Don't include information that you've gone to a particular program for legal nurse consulting training if you are an expert witness, because that looks like you're a hired gun and being an expert witness is your full-time occupation. Would you see a physician put on his or her CV that this person is doing expert work or went to a particular program to learn how to do expert work? It would be unusual to find that. However, if you are presenting yourself as a behind-the-scenes consultant, you might want to stress your legal nurse consulting education.

If you're an expert, don't list the names of the cases that you've worked on. Don't provide the names of the attorneys that you have worked for. This makes it very easy for the opposing counsel to contact those individuals and ask for copies of reports that you've written for them. Opposing counsel may indeed want that information, but make them work for it. Don't give them a path so that they can find it.

What else should you exclude from your resume or curriculum vitae? You don't need a career objective, such as, "Find a job in a progressive labor and delivery unit." That would be appropriate if you were applying for a job, but it's not appropriate if you are looking for expert work.

It's not necessary to include information like birth date, marriage date, names and ages of your children, hobbies, and extra-curricular activities. It's never really possible to anticipate how somebody is going to react to those. In this era of identity theft, be aware of protecting some private details. Do not list your social security number or nursing license number.

If you are a physician, do not list your DEA number.

Don't include stuffing – needless and extraneous details, courses you have taken (but not presented), in other words, everything that you have ever done.

Don't misrepresent your credentials. You've probably read stories about people who have been caught in lies. If you lie about your skills or your background, you're not going to be able to demonstrate them when you're working with attorneys.

Errors

Errors on your resume can be very embarrassing – I've seen a number of resumes with errors in dates or spelling. Carefully proofread your document. Ask someone else to proofread it. Meticulously check the dates. Are they accurate? Do your dates overlap, showing you worked in more than one place at a time? You may have, but be sure the details are accurate.

How many errors do you find in the paragraph below from a resume I received?

∧∧∧∧∧∧∧∧∧∧∧∧∧∧∧∧∧∧∧∧∧∧∧∧∧∧∧∧∧∧

2004 – 2007   Charge Nurse / Sub Acute Care

Carillon Nursing and Rehabilitation Center, Huntington, New York

Developed departmental policy and procedure related to Intravenous therapy management. Staff nurse in chare of patients with cardiac disease, orthopedic injuries and head trauma. Also cared for ophthalmology, neurological, oncology and Alzheimer unit. Reviewed medical records for deviations form established protocols. Responded to code blues throughout facility.

∧∧

Clarity about Degrees

If you are in school working towards a degree, make sure it indicates when you have an expected graduation day. I have seen resumes from a couple of people who were working on degrees who wrote their resumes in a way that implied that they already had the degrees. Make sure that you are truthful about the information and not misleading. Some people add the degree before it is earned, but include a "C" after the degree, as in PhD(c) to indicate they are a candidate for the degree.

Phrases to Avoid

You should avoid certain phrases in your resumes. Here are some examples:

- "I'm an effective communicator." Most of us think we're effective communicators; that doesn't really distinguish you from other people.

- "I'm detail-oriented." Attorneys assume that this is going to be true. You can give an example in your cover letter or in an interview of how you picked up something in medical records that made a difference on a previous case. Include something that happened to you in your job that made a difference, if you haven't done cases yet.

- "References available upon request" is a phrase that's now passé. Always assume that the attorney is going to conduct a web search on you. Pay attention to your social media profile. If you are on LinkedIn or Facebook, remember that you will be projecting an image to people who might be interested in hiring you, so be careful about the pictures that you post.

  I know an expert witness who posted a picture on Facebook of her in a bar drinking a bottle of beer. She was exposing her bra strap for reasons that I don't understand. The picture was time-stamped with 3:20 PM. I called her and said, "Do you really want this on your Facebook page? Do you want opposing counsel to pick up this picture of you and cross-examine you on this in court, even though it's not germane to the case? Think about how you are projecting your image to people." She removed that picture the same afternoon.

- "I'm a team player" – as opposed to being a loner? That's a phrase that you don't need.

- "I can meet deadlines." If you couldn't, how long are you going to last in the field?

Follow conventional formats. Don't organize your document like the table below with columns and rows. Remember that people are used to seeing information written out in a narrative form.

Education:	
10/98	Masters of Science in Physical Therapy

Education:	
10/98	Masters of Science in Physical Therapy Concentration in Biology

Evaluation of Your Resume

Once you have polished your resume or CV, set it aside for a day. When you pick it up again, look at it with an objective eye. Is it a fair representation of your skills? Is it interesting? Is it clear and easy to read? Use the questions below to look at your resume or CV as if you have never seen it before. Based on the information in this chapter, answer these questions. Keep your document current so that you can supply it at a moment's notice to an attorney.

1. Is this a CV or a resume?

2. Does the document contain the basic contact information? Address, email, phone? Is it accurate?

3. Does the document list your work experience with accomplishments?

4. Do you list education and work experience in reverse chronological order? (Include most recent, ending with least recent.)

5. What is your assessment of the design? (Is it easy to read and uncluttered versus crowded?)

6. Did you use a standard font? Is the size readable?

7. Is the format consistent?

8. Does the document contain any of the following: job objective, pictures, personal information, personal references, stuffing, uncommon abbreviations, typographical or grammatical errors, inappropriate email address, or legal nurse consulting training if you are an expert?

It is a good idea to polish your resume or CV using the guidance in this chapter. At least once a year, review the document to make sure it is current.

Types of Nursing Experts

Addiction

Administrators

Ambulatory care

Nurse Anesthetists

Assisted Living

Bariatric

Billing review

Brain injury

Cardiac

Cardiac catheterization

Cardiac rehabilitation

Cardiothoracic

Case management

Chart auditing

Child abuse

Clinical trial nurse

Corrections

Critical care

Developmental disabilities

Dialysis

Emergency medical services

Emergency department

Enterostomal therapy

Faculty

Flight nurses

Genetics

Neuropsychiatric

Group homes

Home health care

Hospice

Infection control

IV Conscious sedation

IV therapy

Labor and delivery

Lactation specialist

Life care planning

Long term care

Long term acute care hospital

Medical surgical

Midwife

Neonatal

Nephrology

Neurosurgical

Newborn

Nurse practitioners:

      Addiction

      Adult

      Critical care

    Emergency department
    Family practice
    Hospitalist
    Internal medicine
    Long term care
    Neonatal
    Neurology
    OB/GYN
    Oncology
    Pediatric
    Psychiatric
    Trauma
Nursing informatics
Obstetrics
Office nurse
Oncology
Operating room
Orthopaedic
Post anesthesia care unit
Pain management
Pediatric oncology
Pediatric rehabilitation
Pediatrics
Pediatric ICU
Pediatric IV therapy
Perioperative
Perivascular
Post partum
Psychiatric

Quality assurance/risk management

Radiology

Rehabilitation

Renal

Respiratory therapy

School nurse

School of nursing administrator

Sexual assault

Sleep disorder

Stroke program

Supervision

Telemetry

Transplant

Trauma

Ultrasound

Wound care

Entering Legal Nurse Consulting as an Expert Witness

Entering Legal Nurse Consulting as an Expert Witness

In the spring of 1987, I sat in a conference room listening to a nurse talk about career alternatives for nurses. I was employed as a nursing quality assurance coordinator and enjoyed the analysis of trends and development of plans to improve care. However, I was traveling 1.25 hours one way a day on the most heavily trafficked roads in New Jersey, and was getting burned out from the trip.

The title of the seminar caught my attention. At that point, I had been out of nursing school for about 20 years and had been a staff nurse, diploma school educator, nursing staff development director, and nursing quality assurance coordinator.

The seminar leader presented information about a number of non-traditional nursing roles. She explained that nurses went to court to testify about standards of care. That sounded very interesting. I had a master's degree in nursing, had coauthored a book about the nursing process, had experience teaching staff nurses and department managers, and liked to write. I had years of staff nurse experience in medical surgical nursing, and maintained clinical involvement while I directed the hospital's staff development department.

The next day when I returned to work, I called the attorney who ran the hospital's risk management department. I asked him how I could get into expert witness work. He explained about my state's jury verdict analysis publication and Martindale Hubbell (now martindale.com) as a way to connect with attorneys.

My life changed forever when I walked into the county courthouse's library. I used the jury verdict analysis publications in the library to determine which attorneys were doing nursing or medical malpractice cases. I copied down information from the volumes of Martindale Hubbell, which was not online at that time, to get the attorneys' contact information. When I had a list of about 20 attorneys, I sent out a letter of introduction explaining that I was available to review medical surgical cases as a nursing expert witness, enclosed my CV, and sat back to see what would happen.

In the meantime, I decided to quit my job. I planned to start a business by piecing together sources of income: consulting with hospitals on quality assurance and documentation issues, being a PRN staff nurse, writing books, and teaching seminars for a national seminar company. I took a leap of faith that was amazing considering that we had faced (but did not have to declare) bankruptcy 5 years earlier when my husband's business failed. That experience, which involved facing the threat of losing our house to satisfy the loans, made me determined to not borrow any money to start a business. (To this day, I have never borrowed money to keep my business going.)

Expert witness work begins

I didn't realize when I sent out those letters that medical surgical units were (and are) frequently the targets of suits. Attorneys needed experts, and lots of them. Experts with my background were not common, and I immediately got the attention of two defense attorneys: one in October 1987 and one in November 1987. The first attorney sent a case that was easy to defend. It involved a young girl who fainted in the bathroom and cut her knee on the smashed glass IV bottle.

I wrote a report that included citations to medical literature. I'd never seen an expert witness report and didn't understand what the attorney needed. Then I got a phone call from him. "Pat, I like your report but the format is wrong. We have to work on that." I revised the report and sent it off.

Within a few months, my client called me, laughing. He said the case was dismissed with prejudice. He explained that after the plaintiff attorney got my report, he took out his checkbook and wrote his client a check and asked her to forget her suit. I found out this was very uncommon and have not heard of it happening since then!

The second attorney who contacted me told me he was defending an LPN who worked on the night shift. An elderly confused man had walked out of the hospital in his patient gown one cold March evening and was knocking on doors in the neighborhood. The police brought him back, and the doctor wrote an order for chest and wrist restraints. The LPN went into the room with the RN who was assigned to him and made sure he was in his chest restraint. The LPN went to attend to her wing of patients. This patient got out of bed within 30 minutes, untied his chest restraint, removed the window screen, walked out onto the hospital roof, and fell into the parking lot in front of the emergency department. He survived his fall and died later from his cancer. The attorney casually mentioned in his November 1987 phone call that trial was set for two months later.

First trial

After I wrote my report defending the LPN, the attorney called me up to discuss scheduling for trial. I remember being floored, and calling a friend in panic. "I wanted to be an expert witness, but I never thought I'd have to testify on the second case I reviewed!"

I think I could have gotten to the courthouse on sheer adrenaline on the day of trial, without needing my car. The defense attorney led me through the direct exam, and then the plaintiff attorney stood up to cross-examine me. I looked at him with dread. He asked only one question: "Was there any documentation that the wrist restraints were placed on the patient?" "No", I told him. When the defense attorney called after the trial was over, I put him on speaker phone, and my husband and son rejoiced to hear that the jury let the LPN off (the RN was held liable, but the award was small.)

That initial batch of twenty letters continued to bring me work, repeat business, and word-of-mouth referrals. My expert witness case load grew.

In 1988, I learned about the American Association of Legal Nurse Consultants (AALNC), a year old at that point. I went to the second annual conference and began learning more about the field. When people asked me what kind of legal nurse consultant I was, I learned to say, "I am an independent LNC and an expert witness."

Expert witness referral business starts Med League Support Services

One day in 1989, a plaintiff attorney asked me to review an emergency department nursing case. "I'm not an ER nurse", I told him, "but I know a masters-prepared clinical specialist who would be great." I connected the two of them, sat back, and the light bulb went off. I had done both of them a favor without any financial compensation. I began to learn more about the process of subcontracting cases to other expert witnesses.

Earlier in my life I had been involved in two multi-level marketing companies. One sold cleaning products; the other sold cosmetics. These companies provided excellent training about sales and business structure. What I clearly learned from those experiences was:

1. Your income is limited by the number of hours you can work. If others are working for you, you can get a piece of other people's hours.

2. When you are marketing, you have to develop a hard shell. Each "no" brings you closer to the person who will say "yes." You learn to say, "Next."

3. I was not destined to sell soap or cosmetics. I knew I could do more with my healthcare background.

After this request for an ER nurse, I formed Med League Support Services as a sole proprietorship. Using the relationships I had built up over the years, I began to recruit nurses to review cases for me. The first expert I got under contract was the ER nurse.

In the beginning, I was casual about supervising experts. However, one day a client called to complain about the semi-literate report he'd received from one of my experts. I was horrified when I saw what she had put together. After that, I insisted that the experts send the reports to me for proofreading. I picked up issues that needed to be resolved before the report could be presented to the attorney and developed resources for training the experts.

Initially, my business was located in my house. We lived at 55 Britton Road, so I added Suite 500 to the address. At first, I had two filing cabinets with a board across the top. My husband and I tried to share a computer. That was short-lived. (He was also running his business out of the house.) Then we turned the family room into my husband's office and put a desk in the living room.

We had two kids under the age of 9. The work day never ended, and I worked all day and into the evening. One day my youngest son, who was 3, asked me for something. Without turning around, I told him (rather self-righteously, I'm afraid) that I could not help him. I was working. He burst into tears and told me, "I feel like such a pest." I decided to hire a part-time employee so I could free up some time.

Moving out

Our decision to get another house resulted from a discussion I had with my spouse in 1996. He said, "Our youngest son does not really need a bedroom. I could use his bedroom for an office." I disagreed. We bought a house 10 miles away and turned the first house into an office house. We had three employees coming in (two of mine, one of his) for two years until a neighbor reported us for violating the zoning rules. Fortunately, we had already made an offer—which was accepted—to purchase a 3,600 square feet office condo. The zoning officer took pity on us and did not close our businesses down. Within a month, we had moved out of the office house into the office condo. My husband and I bought the condo and rented it to our businesses. The rent we took paid for the condo three times over.

Federal Rule of Evidence 1006

I reviewed cases as a testifying liability expert for 20 years and enjoyed just about every aspect of the role (except cross-examination). Shortly after I started reviewing cases as an expert, in around 1990, one of my clients asked me to summarize records of a man who had a botched laparoscopic cholecystectomy. He developed a fistula that leaked bile which digested his abdomen. There were no nursing liability issues involved; my client wanted me to explain to the jury what this deceased patient went through. I remember testifying by sharing poignant quotes from the record and looking over to see tears pouring down his wife's face.

There was no name for this role of explaining medical records when I first began performing it and it was uncommon in my state until a judge endorsed it. The role is now variously called pain and suffering expert, expert fact witness or expert witness or Rule 1006 expert.

Building a Successful Legal Nurse Consulting Practice

Here are some strategies you can implement to create a strong legal nurse consulting business.

1. If at all possible, create your business launch so that you are not under pressure to make a profit right away. It takes more time than you would expect to market and start attracting clients. When I started Med League, my husband was bringing in enough money that I could take my time building my business. I got income from teaching seminars, consulting with hospitals and performing expert witness work. Gradually I centered on working with attorneys as my primary source of income.

2. Learn the nuances of marketing and writing appealing copy for brochures and websites. Your prospect is bombarded with information. You have to capture that person's attention quickly and in a compelling way. I have studied this aspect of running a business and invested thousands of dollars in courses and books to learn more about marketing. The more you understand about marketing, the more comfortable and confident you feel.

3. Pick the right service that fits your strengths. If you have a broad base of nursing, you are in an ideal position to help attorneys understand nursing malpractice cases. If you have only worked critical care, and con-

tinue to maintain a clinical practice, you may be in an ideal position to testify as an expert witness on critical care cases. Know what you are good at and recognize that it cannot be at all aspects of running a business or legal nurse consulting. Find others to help you.

4. Recognize that you need a solid foundation in clinical nursing to be able to work most effectively with attorneys. Understanding how a hospital runs is invaluable in assisting attorneys. Nurses who have experience only in non-hospital roles are going to find it tougher to perform some aspects of legal nurse consulting.

5. Be aware of the advantages and disadvantages of working on cases for attorneys who could swamp your firm with volume. For example, a multidistrict litigation case could become the elephant that pushes out the time you have for attorneys who send you one case at a time. When my LNC business worked on a large multidistrict litigation case, our regular clients noticed the longer turnaround for their cases. We were on a continuous treadmill of churning out reports and were relieved when the cases finally wound down.

6. Never stop marketing. Your primary client could have a sudden change in practice due to a change in the law, or could leave the firm, or drop dead.

7. Pay attention to relationships. Your clients want to work with LNCs they know, like, and trust. There is a lot at stake in a lawsuit - a lot of time, money, and effort. Look for ways to build strong relationships with your clients so that they would not dream of working with another independent LNC firm. Advise them when you come across a case like theirs that has been settled or tried, and share the result. Be flexible when possible with payment plans. One client of ours was frank with us that his client was responsible for the fees and could

not pay the bill, nor could the attorney. Our client told us, "Be flexible with me, and I'll make it up to you." He remained a loyal client who paid his bills for more than a decade.

8. Use honest and ethical business practices. Return unused portions of retainers, keep detailed billing records, and always check for a conflict of interest before accepting a case. A legal vendor I know told me that she only returns unused portions of a retainer if the client asks for them. That strikes me as dishonest. You have to be able to look yourself in the mirror and be proud of your ethics.

9. Avoid borrowing money if you can. Use your revenues, not loans, to invest in your business such as upgrading your computer equipment. When my husband started his welding business in 1980, we borrowed a million dollars and signed personal guarantees for the amount. When his business failed two years later, we were on the hook for a million that we did not have. I was pregnant with our second child when a man came from the bank to evaluate our house to determine if it was worth taking to satisfy some of the debt. My husband's keen negotiating skills kept us from having to declare bankruptcy.

10. Charge reasonable fees that the market will bear. Do not join the rush to the bottom to undercut your competitors. You will destroy your business by performing work at the lowest rate on the market, find it impossible to raise fees, and run out of money. One man called me a few years ago to ask if I wanted to bid on doing medical summaries. He quoted a price he had heard from another company, which was half of our hourly rate, and asked if I could do better. I wanted to ask him, "Do better for ourselves or for you?" I explained we could

not do the work for that rate. Another firm asked us to work on pharmaceutical product liability cases, and wait until the cases settled to get paid. I refused, saying we could not ask our subcontractors to wait to get paid; I was unwilling to go into debt to pay them before we got paid. Think through the financial consequences of taking these kinds of arrangements.

11. Charge rush fees. Determine what will constitute a rush rate, with a specific time frame, and adhere to that rate. My company charged our clients and paid our nursing experts a rush rate when they were expected. to produce work on a short turnaround. I resisted rush rates for years, fearing it would cause us to lose business. I found attorneys expected to pay rush fees.

12. Consider the multiple ways you can reach your market: a website, a blog, tweets, Facebook, ezines, emails, videos, and video testimonials. Use these methods to remind your client base of your existence. Use principles of crafting effective marketing messages and consistently implement them.

13. Leverage your time and talent. You will build a stronger business if you use subcontractors. Hire people who have particular expertise in an area you lack, such as a different type of clinical nursing, to review cases for you. This is a better use of your time than trying to master the nuances of a different area of nursing.

14. Train your subcontractors well. Explain your expectations, give them sample work product, review their samples, and be quick to correct and reject those who are not capable of doing the work.

15. "Hire slowly, fire quickly." There is a great deal of wisdom in that expression. Carefully screen employees. A typo on a resume is enough for me to set it aside. I have fired employees for absenteeism, incompetence, and poor attitude. Be grateful when a marginal employee quits. Although it causes short term disruption, it is far better for a person to self-select out of your system. Don't tolerate marginal work performance. There are far better people looking for work.

16. Use financial controls in your business. Avoid providing embezzlement and theft opportunities. When you have employees, have one person open the mail and another person deposit the money. Do not allow employees to sign checks; no one should be able to sign except for the owner. (One of my colleagues caught an employee buying a personal computer charged to the company credit card. The employee counted on the owner not looking at the credit card bill. It was a fluke that the owner saw the bill and caught the purchase.) Allow only extremely trustworthy employees to access bank accounts. Be very careful about allowing employees to remotely access your server. Someone could secure a laptop or desktop computer in an employee's home and gain access to the company's data. And if that employee quits or gets fired, how will you keep your data safe?

17. Your employees are not your friends. Do not be overly generous. Be fair, be aware of the labor laws, and be careful with benefits and bonuses.

18. Recognize that there is a lot of competition in the legal nurse consulting field. What can you do to set yourself apart? What is your competitive advantage? How can you stand out in a crowded field? Determine your strengths and weaknesses and develop a plan for building on your strengths and compensating for your weaknesses.

19. Recognize the value of being published and of being connected to other legal nurse consultants. My career was immensely helped by my active role in editing textbooks and serving on the AALNC board of directors for 5 years, including a term as president. Although it was a huge time commitment, it helped me establish many lasting relationships and learn more about board dynamics and the differences between running a national organization and running a small business.

20. Starting a business is hard and not for everyone. Be prepared to sacrifice, to work long hours and to continuously learn. Entrepreneurship gets into your blood as you begin to experience the joys of being your own boss.

After growing the company to the point of consistently hitting 7-figure annual sales, I decided to look for a buyer. Although I tried on my own to locate a buyer, I was not successful until I hired a business broker. He worked with me to develop a package to present to potential buyers. What I learned to emphasize is that the company was not me. It did not rest on my skills. My company had 200 expert witnesses under contract to review cases, a robust private training site for our experts, a large database of repeat clients, and a steady stream of cases. It had solid cash flow and provided me as the owner with a significant amount of compensation. I built an appealing legacy business.

Following a year of working with the business broker, being interviewed by a few dozen prospects and receiving several offers, I sold Med League on January 2, 2015. It was a tremendous feeling to know that the work I did to build the company would continue to help others, including the new owner, employees, subcontractors and clients. Now I work with legal nurse consultants who want to get more clients, make more money and avoid expensive mistakes. Get details at **www.LNCacademyinc.com.**

Mastering the Expert Witness Role

Mastering the Expert Witness Role

Serving as an Expert Witness is an Important Commitment

During my many years of both serving as an expert witness and supervising the hundreds of expert witnesses under contract to my former business, I've learned a number of principles that will help you in this position.

You may think the following goes without saying, but it's a point worth reiterating. When you agree to review a case as an expert, it's not a casual decision. It's a serious commitment to the attorney and his or her client. They rely on your expertise and dependability. Once you are named as the expert on a case, you can't casually change your mind.

Consider the following questions before accepting a case:

1. Do you have the experience and expertise to review the case?

2. Do you have the time to review the case and meet the attorney's deadlines?

3. Are you willing to write a report if the attorney requests it?

4. Are you willing to testify at deposition and/or trial if the case moves forward?

If you can't answer with an unequivocal "yes" to any of these questions, make the ethical choice. Don't agree to be the expert on the case.

After the attorney names you as an expert on a case, you won't find it easy to resign from this role. Once you have submitted a report, you may be deposed or asked to testify at trial as part of your commitment to your role. When you have written a report, you have made an almost irrevocable commitment.

Attorneys are often working under deadlines and/or statutes of limitations. Once they name you as their expert, you put the case at risk of being lost if you change your mind. The attorney usually doesn't have time to start all over again with another expert. Doing so makes the attorney and client spend even more money for a new expert.

In addition, there's no guarantee that another expert will agree with your opinion. This would be a very bad situation for the attorney.

Offering to waive your fee if you leave the case is not an option and does not provide you with the right to leave the case.

I urge you to approach being an expert on a case as a tremen-dous opportunity *and* a huge responsibility. Engage in your work with professionalism and commitment. The attorney and his client are counting on you.

How Your Performance as an Expert Witness is Judged

Once you've agreed to take on the role of expert witness, attorneys, judges, or an agency that contracts for your services will evaluate your performance according to certain vital elements. I describe them briefly below and will cover them in greater detail in other parts of this book.

When you receive materials from an attorney, call his/her office to acknowledge the receipt. The support staff who have assembled these materials will appreciate this.

Always promptly return the attorney's or paralegal's calls. If you don't, they will worry and will probably call to find out why you didn't respond. They will remember the failure to respond, which will reflect on your reputation for reliability.

Another item in the promptness menu is the prompt submis-sion of invoices. This helps you to be paid as soon as possible.

Make your bills reasonable. If you are starting your career as an expert witness, you can't bill for time spent learning new skills. For example, it may take you longer than it takes an experienced expert to review materials. Only as you gain confidence, will you realize that you don't have to read every page of the medical record and can scan other materials.

You are judged by the quality of your report. Write a report that's thoughtful, concise, covers the major points, is well written, and carefully proofread. (Refer to *How to Analyze Medical Records: A Primer for Legal Nurse Consultants*, for specific details on how to polish your report. This book is Book 3 in the **Creating a Successful LNC Practice Series** available at **www.legalnursebusiness.com**.)

In a report for the plaintiff, focus on significant deviations. Explain the standard of care and how the nurses deviated from it. Use legally correct language.

In a report for the defense, address the allegations of the plaintiff's expert or the complaint filed in the suit. Explain why the nurses met the standard of care. State you hold these opinions to a reasonable degree of nursing probability.

Here are additional ways you are judged as an expert witness:

Not only do you meet deadlines, you turn in reports and opinions before their due dates. This reduces attorneys' stress about deadlines, and they will remember you in a very positive way.

You have well-organized material such that you can find a document within seconds. This assists you in every stage of the case, from record review, report preparation, deposition preparation and testimony, and trial preparation and testimony.

You are well-organized, being thoroughly familiar with your report and the materials before your deposition begins. At your deposition, you hold to your opinion, avoid the various traps the opposing attorney will try to set for you, and resist being bulldozed.

You are equally well prepared at the trial. You know the facts, clearly express your opinions, look at the jury when testifying, and maintain your composure under cross-examination.

Types of Experts

Life Care Planners

Life care planners perform detailed analysis of a plaintiff's current and future medical needs and costs. This information is used to achieve a just settlement or verdict once liability and causation are established. Life care planners need to organize material, prepare reports, and testify at deposition or trial. They are typically nurses, although other healthcare professionals also serve in this role.

Expert Fact Witness/Pain and Suffering Expert/ Damages Expert

Damages experts are also known by various names, such as *expert fact witness or pain and suffering witness.* The terms "expert fact witness" or "pain and suffering expert" are not standard legal ones. The role is allowed under the Federal Rules of Evidence Rule 1006 – to provide a summary of voluminous medical records, using medical expertise.

Experts who explain medical records and details of care are expert witnesses. They are witnesses who rely on special skills: to be able to read and interpret medical records and to synthesize and summarize that information in an objective manner in order to communicate what a plaintiff went through after an injury occurred. The damages expert prepares a detailed written report, gets deposed, and testifies at trial.

The witness typically uses laymen's terms to explain the medical records, the injuries, the medicine, the nursing care, and what happened to the plaintiff. This testimony is not opinion-based. The expert serves on the basis of expertise, skill, education, and training.

Although this role is specifically allowed within the Federal Rules of Evidence, it is not utilized as much as it could be. (Attorneys and LNCs are much more familiar with the roles of liability experts who evaluate information to determine if the standard of care was followed.) Although physicians can provide this type of testimony, attorneys may hire nurses because it is more cost effective particularly in a large case.

I spent 20 years reviewing cases as a liability expert witness and testified in several hundred depositions and trials. I began reviewing cases as a damages expert in 1987 and as a Rule 1006 expert in 1990.

Liability Expert Witness

According to *Black's Law Dictionary*, the liability nursing expert witness is a person who, through education or experience, has developed skill or knowledge in a particular subject matter so that he or she may form an opinion that will assist the fact finder. The expert analyzes information, may prepare a written report (based on the state's rules), may be deposed (based on the state's rules), and testifies at trial.

Expert Qualifications

What does it take to do well as an expert witness? Do you qualify to review this case by virtue of your education, training, and experience? Sometimes expert witnesses are asked these questions in a very confrontational way during a deposition.

"What makes you think you're an expert?"

You have to be able to defend yourself and answer that question in a credible and logical way. If you are asked in a deposition why you think you are an expert, how would you defend yourself?

Typically experts draw their strength from these factors:

- *Education* - ideally the expert is well educated. An advanced degree in nursing is desirable. The expert should have a minimum of an Associate's degree, a Bachelors, or ideally a Master's degree.

- *Training* – ideally the expert is clinically certified in a subspecialty of nursing. The person has received specialized training in this aspect of nursing.

- *Experience* - the expert is well-experienced in the clinical care in question. Some states require an active clinical practice within a certain number of years of the incident. If you are unsure, ask the attorney about regulations in that state.

I qualified these statements with the term "ideally" because there are well-qualified experts thoroughly grounded in the clinical issues of a case who do not have a degree or certification. However, when pitted against an expert on the other side who has both the degrees and certification, the first expert may look less qualified.

Federal Rules of Evidence Rule 702 Testimony by Expert Witnesses

Federal rule define the requirements for an expert to ground opinions in knowledge. Rule 702 states:

A witness who is qualified as an expert by knowledge, skill, experience, training, or education may testify in the form of an opinion or otherwise if:

    (a) the expert's scientific, technical, or other specialized knowledge will help the trier of fact to understand the evidence or to determine a fact in issue;

    (b) the testimony is based on sufficient facts or data;

    (c) the testimony is the product of reliable principles and methods; and

    (d) the expert has reliably applied the principles and methods to the facts of the case.

The Federal Rules of Evidence define the background of an expert witness. The Federal Rules of Evidence apply to federal cases, such as when the company is located in a different state and is being sued by another attorney in a different state from where the company is located. If that company has national offices, it may become a federal case, depending on the circumstances.

The Federal Rules of Evidence are copied by many states. There might be a rule of evidence in your state that is worded very closely to or identically to the Rule 702. This rule stresses that the testimony should be based on sufficient facts or data. There should be a credible analysis of the information (not that expert's personal theory) which is supported by a body of literature or the standard of care.

Composure

Experts should be poised and not easily perturbed. They should be able to withstand aggressive cross examination and questioning. I know an expert who was shattered during a deposition. She called me while she was driving home. I instructed her to pull over because she was sobbing. We agreed after we finished talking that she would be allowed to withdraw from the case after I talked to the attorney. I have never seen someone so devastated.

Objectivity

Experts should be objective and evenly balanced, if possible, with numbers of plaintiff and defense cases. Many feel that the ideal expert has an equal number of defense and plaintiff cases.

Once when I was looking for an expert witness, I had two separate conversations with two different nursing experts who did not want to take a case on behalf of the plaintiff. They wanted to only do defense cases. I explained the issues that come up when an expert will only review cases on one side. I was not able to dissuade these individuals from refusing the case, and I think ultimately they will find that they would be better served showing objectivity by reviewing cases on both sides.

Skeletons in the Closet

The expert should have no skeletons in the closet. I asked a series of questions of anyone I was thinking of getting under contract to review cases as an expert. Termination from a job, suspension of license, or having been sued are all factors that send up a warning flag. Ideally, the expert has not been personally sued for nursing malpractice. A few of the nursing expert witnesses may have been involved in suits as administrators of their facilities. I would screen out anyone who had been a defendant in a suit and lost the suit.

The importance of a background check came home in a case in which I was a defense nursing expert. The case involved a woman who fell in the bathroom. The plaintiff expert was a nurse who had a chronic illness. The defense attorney contacted the Board of Nursing and asked for the record of this individual. He was asked by the Board of Nursing, "Would you like her *disciplinary* record too?"

The attorney found out she had been disciplined, and her license had been suspended. She had been caught writing prescriptions to herself for Vicodin using her husband's prescription pad and forging his signature. She did this 22 times. In her deposition, she claimed no memory of having done it, but the Board of Nursing records were rather clear. The judge allowed the jury to hear about this background. It certainly damaged her credibility, and she was judged accordingly by the jury. The defense won the case.

The expert puts *nothing* on social media that he or she would not want to see on a blow-up in the courtroom.

Consistency

The expert holds consistent opinions. Prior reports and publications support the expert's opinions. I have been cross-examined on information that I have written in my textbooks.

Income

The expert does not rely on expert witness work for a major portion of his or her income. Consider how much income you gain by being an expert witness. It should be ideally a minimal part of your total income. Those experts who make their living testifying and writing reports are vulnerable to charges that they're hired guns who will testify for anyone at any time. Some states' rules allow attorneys to get information from the expert about her total income and even to request tax returns.

Nurses Evaluate Nurses

Nursing experts review only nursing care. They're not evaluating physician care. On occasion when I was proofreading reports of experts, I found nursing experts who are critical of the physician involved in the situation. You can predict how the cross-examination would go.

Nurse, did you go to medical school?
No.

Are you board certified in this aspect of medicine?
No.

Are you certified in any aspect of medicine?
No.

The dilemma in analyzing cases is that clinical nurses have to know enough of the standard of care to be able to question a physician who does not respond in the appropriate or the expected way. That's our professional obligation, but the courts do not allow us to testify about the standard of care for physicians.

It is well known that legal nurse consultants are retained by attorneys to evaluate a case to give a screening opinion about physician performance according to the standard of care. As LNCs, we are perfectly qualified to do literature searches, look at the medical records, put the pieces of the evidence together, and form the initial opinion to help the plaintiff attorney or the defense attorney get some sense of direction on the case. But nursing expert witnesses are not allowed to present opinions about physician standard of care.

Nurses are retained by defense attorneys who are representing a physician. They may, as part of their strategy, ask the nurse to look at the nursing care to deflect blame away from the physician and onto the nurses. They're hired by the defense, but they're acting in what you would ordinarily think of as a plaintiff role.

Physicians Evaluate Physicians

Physicians should not be evaluating nursing care. This is less and less common, but I occasionally hear of physicians who are asked to form opinions about nursing care. The physician would be vulnerable to questions:

Are you a registered nurse? Did you go to nursing school? Are you a member of any professional nursing associations? Are you certified in any aspect of nursing?"

MASTERING THE EXPERT WITNESS ROLE

Nursing has its own unique body of knowledge, standards and regulations, and practice acts that are independent of physicians.

In a case called Sullivan vs. Edwards Hospital in Illinois in 2004, a physician was the only expert. The physician opined about the nursing standard of care. The Association of Nurse Attorneys weighed in on this, as did other groups, and objected to the use of a physician to comment on nursing standard of care. They were able to successfully argue that the attorney for the plaintiff was required to have a nurse as his expert and not a physician.

A Real-Life Illustration
An expert submitted a report to an attorney with two significant errors. The first was criticizing the physician; the second was stating that the deviations caused the patient's problem. I've changed the details in the segment below. However, the errors are real.

The expert wrote: "The medical records indicate that Dr. Bloomfield and Nurses R. Jones R.N. and E. Marcus R.N. deviated from standards of care when treating Mrs. Tanner on 11/20/15. The nurses deviated by.... Dr. Bloomfield deviated by failing to recognize the signs of fetal distress and failing to arrange for a cesarean section within 30 minutes. These failures caused the infant to develop hypoxic brain damage and cerebral palsy."

This report damaged the expert's credibility, required preparation of a new report, and impeded her ability to collect the money owed for the work performed.

In summary, don't criticize doctors. If questioned in a deposition, say you're not there to comment on the physician standard of care. Don't offer opinions on causation. It's the attorney's job to hire a physician to address this subject if the facts of the case warrant it.

Initial Steps

As the expert, you've gotten a phone call from an attorney who asked about reviewing a case. Most of the time the case shows up with a phone call first as opposed to walking in the door, but on occasion an expert may receive records from an attorney's office without any prior notice. I always think that's a little risky on the part of the attorney because the nurse might be already involved in the case in some other way.

The first thing to do is to verify that there is no conflict of interest. You would not be considered objective if you took a case involving your own hospital system or one of your friends or relatives. Do you know the plaintiff or defendant? Anything that would impair objectivity would not make you a desirable expert.

The next thing is to find out what the attorney is asking of you. Is it to provide a screening opinion? Is it to be a testifying expert?

Occasionally experts say, "I'll be happy to review it, but I will not go to court. I would not testify. Testifying is too disruptive to my schedule. I don't want to do it." Ninety-nine percent of the time when the attorney wants an expert, he or she expects that person to be able to go to court to testify if the expert can support the attorney's position. Although testimony can be provided through videotape, many people feel this is a little less effective than having the expert in the courtroom. (This leads to the interesting question of, "Will you come live?" We know that means in person, but my brain fills in, "As opposed to dead?")

Attorneys occasionally attempt to pressure the expert for an opinion in the initial phone call. "What do you think? Based on what I told you, tell me what you think." I understand that attorneys are trying to avoid retaining experts who will not support their case, but it is often very difficult, if not impossible, to offer any opinions over the phone without seeing the records.

Sometimes when you're starting out as an expert witness, you may be eager to get cases. The work may be coming in slowly. Make sure that you only take cases that are within your area of expertise. You must be confident about it because that will carry over into the way you testify and present yourself. The more confident you are and the surer you are, the more the attorneys will recognize that. This includes not only the attorney you're working with but the opposing attorney. I received several cases from attorneys who took my deposition and then asked me to review cases for them.

Beware the Crafty Plaintiff

If a plaintiff approaches you directly, make it clear that he or she needs to connect you with the attorney involved in the case. This cautionary tale explains why.

An expert received a subtly worded email: "I have been asked to locate an expert witness to review a case involving a woman who suffered from a sudden air embolism. I am helping the attorney who is handling the case. I would like to discuss retaining a nursing expert witness with expertise in IV therapy. Please supply the CV and fee schedule of the appropriate expert." The sender was (name changed) Fred Wright, ABF Consulting Company.

The expert assumed that Fred was a legal nurse consultant who was hired to help the attorney. She contacted Fred, who asked if she had 30-60 minutes to discuss the woman's case. Not realizing who Fred was and also making the mistake of not requesting advance payment, she made arrangements to meet him in a hotel lobby the next day.

The expert expended an hour of travel time and 30 minutes on a meeting with Fred, who brought one page of medical records. The records stated that his *wife* had died of a pulmonary embolism, not an air embolism, as he believed. He wanted the expert to supply him with any autopsy reports from air embolism cases that she had reviewed and wasn't happy when she said she couldn't do this.

However, he provided his credit card information. When she ran the charge, the card was declined. She asked him for another form of payment for the $337.50 due. Although she made it clear that the fee agreement included travel time, which was billed at the same rate as the consultation time, Fred vigorously argued about the travel time charge and agreed only to pay for the half-hour meeting. He ultimately sent her a check for it.

The lessons you can take forward from this experience are: Get absolute clarity on whom you're talking to. Ask the name of the attorney or nurse legal expert involved in the case. Send out a written form that defines the financial terms of agreement.

If you have any reason to question the authenticity of a caller, investigate further.

Intake Form

I recommend using a standard intake form, which you may wish to modify as you develop experience in gathering information. A standard intake form helps you gather the information that you need in order to be able to determine if you can assist the attorney. Here are some of the important components.

At the top of the form provide room for the law firm, phone number, and email address. Include a referral source on the form. You want to be able to thank the people who are directing work towards your business. If you have advertised, it's useful to know whether the person who's inquiring about the services came as a result of an advertisement for your services.

Identify whether this person is a prospect (new to you) or a client (has already given you work). Is the person you are talking to a paralegal or an attorney? Which side does that person represent – plaintiff or defense? What are the names of the patient and the defendant? (Use the patient's name as the key piece of data rather than the plaintiff, because they are not always the same.)

Check for a conflict of interest before you hear any details of the case. Check your database to be sure you're not already involved in the case for the opposing side. Then take notes about the issue identifying what the attorney's concerns are, and make sure you are an expert in the specific clinical issues of the case.

Knowing the deadline is very important. Is this something that has to be turned around by next Thursday? Is this something that is brand new? Is this something with a tight deadline? What specifically does the attorney need by the deadline?

A form to be filled out?

A report?

A verbal opinion?

Set up a series of items to check off that guide you through the next steps. Typically they are:

- Send a fee agreement with a retainer request

- Send your resume or C.V.

- Log the possible case into your database

I recommend getting a retainer equal to 10 hours of work. A retainer is a good idea from a cash flow perspective, and it enables you to have assurance that you're going to be paid for your initial work.

Tips for Organization

Color Coding
There are four systems which help keep you organized: color coding, file naming, a database, and an inquiry log.

I recommend using color-coded file folders. Types of cases might include expert witness cases for plaintiff attorneys, cases subcontracted out to other nursing experts on behalf of the plaintiff, expert work done for defense attorneys and cases subcontracted out to defense nursing experts.

You will find it much easier to locate folders with a color scheme. I also recommend color coding billing sheets. You could use one color for nurses and another for support staff. Color coding billing sheets makes them stand out in a stack of white paper.

File Naming

You will find it imperative to have a clearly labeled and organized way to keep records. Here is a system that has worked for me. It is based on an assumption that you have a physical file for each case. You may also chose to be paperless and scan documents as they come to you. Whether you have a physical file or an electronic file or both, use a consistent method of naming your file folder tree. Put three names on every file: the law firm name, the attorney name, and the patient name. Let's say Robert Harris of Watson and Harris sent you records to review involving a patient named Tom Billings. You would name the file Watson/Harris/Billings. Write these three names on the file. Save the case information on your server in a folder created for the Watson and Harris firm. The file would contain a folder for Harris, Robert. Inside, you would find a file called Billings, Tom. You won't lose files when you use a system that is logical to you.

Database

I strongly advise you to have a contact management system – a database – to keep track of your cases and clients. Refer to

Patricia Iyer, *How to Start a Legal Nurse Consulting Business*, at **www.nurselegalbusiness.com** to learn more about setting up a database. This is Book 1 in the series, **Creating a Successful LNC Practice**. Keep each client and each case in a database so you can quickly check for a conflict of interest when an attorney contacts you about a new case.

Inquiry Log

Keep track of your incoming calls with an inquiry log. The log is a table that includes the date, name of the attorney, and name of the case. Record each new inquiry in this logbook. It's a very quick way of identifying which cases are open, meaning they haven't come in. Use the log to make calls to check on the case status.

Also, I recommend calling the attorney the day after you email your credentials and fee schedule. A surprising number of emails get caught in a spam filter and never reach the attorney.

Taming the File

The first step when the records come in is to put them in some semblance of order. As soon as you put two legal nurse consultants together for any length of time, you hear stories about medical records that come in very disorganized. Sometimes they look like they were thrown up in the air and then put into a stack with no rhyme or reason.

I'm not always sure if disorganized records come that way from the hospital or nursing home or if they get scattered in the attorney's office. It requires a skilled person to put them together in a logical way so that it's easy to find information.

The only really reliable way to find out if records are missing is to divide them into subsections. See *How to Analyze Medical Records: A Primer for Legal Nurse Consultants*, which is Book 3 in **Creating a Successful LNC Practice Series**. It has an entire chapter on organizing medical records. Get it at **www.legalnursebusiness.com**.

As you're looking at the records, whether that may be as an expert or as a consultant, some of the questions that come up involve whether or not the records are consistent or inconsistent. Is there information that just doesn't add up that's documented one way in one section and a different way in another section? It is not common, but it will happen to you that you will get charts which contain medical records of other patients, not the one who's involved in the lawsuit.

What is the defendant's role if you're on the defense side? Did the plaintiff attorney name several nurses involved in providing care to the plaintiff, or did the plaintiff attorney focus in on specific individuals?

Are there any alterations in the medical record? This is something that as a legal nurse consultant you should always bring to the attention of the attorney, who may be unaware of the alterations. They could be really crucial to a case. Refer to Patricia Iyer and Barbara Levin, *Medical Legal Aspects of Medical Records*, Second Edition, for a chapter I coauthored on tampering with medical records. This book is available at **www.legalnursebusiness.com**.

Documentation plays a critical role in nursing malpractice cases. Experts heavily rely on what the nurses wrote at the time of care. You may see a chart with glaring holes in charting. You may see a chart that is very well documented with no boxes left unchecked, no opportunities for wondering whether something was done or not, and yet there's a horrible result, such as an extensive pressure sore.

4 Elements of Medical Malpractice Suit

Duty

Duty is often the easiest element to prove in a medical malpractice case. Was there a duty between the healthcare provider and the patient? If you were in a restaurant and saw somebody clutch his chest and fall off of his chair, you don't have a relationship with that person. You have no duty to run over and see if you can be of help, but if you do go over, you are expected to provide the appropriate level of care.

Breach of Duty

Expert witnesses are most heavily involved in analyzing the question of a breach of duty. Experts use the standard of care to evaluate this. I will provide more information of sources of standards of care later in the chapter.

Damages

Is there an injury? Most plaintiff attorneys would not take a case without substantial damages. The injuries are typically significant and permanent. They are also usually visible injuries.

Causation

Can we connect the care that was given or not given with the outcome? This is traditionally the role of the physician expert.

Handling Records

Here are some of the guidelines on managing records. Some expert witnesses take notes. Depending on state law, the notes may be discoverable. Many people put Post-it notes on key pages of the medical record. I find that system to be helpful. Do not highlight on the medical record or on the depositions. I saw a deposition transcript in which someone in the law firm drew a huge circle around some testimony and highlighted it in yellow and said, "Pay attention to this". You do not want to sit in a deposition having to explain the note and big circle. Avoid highlighting, circling, or writing comments in the margin on the medical records.

If you prepare a chronology, it could be discoverable. Some attorneys want their experts to provide a chronology. Some do not want a chronology or are not willing to pay for one. It is important to clarify whether you should prepare a chronology.

Deciphering words in medical records, particularly hand-written words, can be very challenging. Words that you cannot decipher may come back to haunt you. It's possible to enlarge a document with a photocopier, zoom in, and have another person take a look at it. Do the best job that you can to decipher the medical record.

Sources of Standards of Care

These are some sources that expert witnesses may use to establish the standard of care.

- Literature current at the time

- Institutional policies and procedures (which are obtainable by the plaintiff attorney only after suit is filed)

- The Joint Commission standards
- State and federal regulations
- Standards of professional organizations such as ones with healthcare providers as members
- State practice act

Verbal Reporting of Findings

You may get into the materials and find that there are pages missing. Maybe somebody copied every other page in the medical record. Maybe somebody put medical records in a box under a secretary's desk and forgot that they were part of what needed to go out to the expert. It is your job to make sure that everything is complete before offering an opinion and talking to the attorney about the pros and cons.

Typically, the next thing that happens is that you have a phone call with the attorney to talk about the initial conclusions after reviewing all of the relevant information. This is an opportunity for you to demonstrate your clinical experience, education, and expertise.

Sometimes you will be reporting to a paralegal or legal nurse consultant, but more typically you will be commenting directly to the attorney. Sometimes attorneys become so convinced of the righteousness of their case that they become blind to another way of looking at it. It's your job to look at it objectively, to see the pros and the cons, and to be able to help the attorney anticipate what the other side is going to say about this particular case.

Going forward with a weak case does a disservice to all the parties, so it's important that you feel strongly about the liability or the defensibility of this case, depending on which side you are on.

Depositions

Purpose of a Deposition
The expert's preliminary evaluation of a case's merits can alter after reading depositions. The purpose of a deposition is to determine the credibility of not only the defendant but of fact witnesses (those who have knowledge of the events but are not named as defendants.)

Basically, a deposition involves giving sworn testimony before a court reporter. Sometimes a fact witness's answers result in being named as a defendant. For example, if a nurse testifies that she didn't report an observed change in a patient's condition to a doctor, she may end up as a defendant in the lawsuit. For these reasons, reviewing a deposition transcript is an important job.

Review of Defendant Depositions
If you receive a deposition transcript from an attorney, contact him or her to find out what is requested. Some attorneys regularly send depositions to experts with a cover letter asking you to call with your thoughts. Others may send a series of depositions simultaneously. The cover letter will tell you what to do next. Always ask for the full transcripts. A summary of a deposition prepared by the law firm may leave out important details.

The attorney may want you to do any of the following:

- Look for discrepancies in the testimony of the deponent. These discrepancies may occur when the witness contradicts herself or the testimony of someone else.

- Also see whether testimony supports or conflicts with your opinions.

- Be on the alert for references to documents you don't have that you may want to request.

- Determine if the defendants contradict each others' descriptions of an event.

Sometimes deposition testimony reveals fuller descriptions of practices. These might not match the standard of care. For example, in one case of a patient who hemorrhaged in a same-day recovery area, the expert suspected that the same-day surgery nurse hadn't taken a set of vital signs when a patient entered her unit. The nurse confirmed this in her testimony. She had copied the last set of vital signs from the recovery room, which was the usual practice of same-day surgery nurses.

Don't write on the deposition transcripts because you will be asked about your written notes if you're deposed. Flag the most important pages with post it notes and remove it (post it notes) when you've finished preparing for your own deposition.

Other Reasons for Reading Depositions
When the plaintiff expert reads the defense expert's reports, he or she can anticipate some of the questions that may be asked in his/her deposition. Typically, the plaintiff expert witness is deposed before the defense expert.

Read the opposing expert's deposition. Notice how the opposing expert has taken the same facts and viewed them differently. Discern weaknesses in the expert's position or background or facts that were ignored. You might find that the expert has a weak clinical background, or overlooked documentation supporting your position in the case.

After you review the depositions, review the medical records to see whether you've changed or expanded your opinions about the case. Be ready to concisely describe your responses to the deposition(s).

If appropriate, recommend that the attorney ask for additional documents, such as policies and procedures. Also ask the attorney about any depositions you may not have received. Sometimes they add nothing to the body of information, but reading everything available is part of your preparation for court. To not have read one and then be cross-examined about it damages your credibility.

Once you've received all the depositions, the attorney may ask you to prepare a report. Refer to your review of the medical records and depositions, as well as other documents you received, to do so. The next chapter delves into this topic and gives you tips to make your reports shine.

Crafting Expert Witness Reports

Crafting Expert Witness Reports

An expert witness' report is a crucial document within the legal arena. It should clearly define opinions. The report will follow the expert throughout the litigation process – from depositions to the courtroom. The report will surface in other cases and be used to try to trap the expert.

It is also an important document in terms of marketing your skills as an expert. It will be evaluated by attorneys and others who determine if they want to give you a chance or pass you by.

Expert witnesses are asked to prepare reports in these situations:

- The expert is completing an affidavit of merit or a certificate of merit in a state that requires it for the initiation of litigation.

- The expert can support the opinion of the attorney who retained him or her, and the attorney has requested a written report expressing opinions.

- The expert cannot support the opinion of the attorney and is asked to prepare a report to share with the client (plaintiff or insurance carrier).

In some venues, no one writes a report; it's not required. In others, the attorney talks to the expert and provides a summary of the expert's opinions. In some areas the report has to detail specific deviations alleged (or refuted, in the case of a defense expert). In some states the regulations hold the expert to "the four corners of the report". This means that once the expert has written the report, he or she is held accountable for those opinions. It is difficult to modify initial opinions. The opinions can be supplemented as time goes on.

There is a great deal of regional variation. Consider the New York Metropolitan area.

- In *New Jersey*, expert reports are required on all cases. There are very strict guidelines about people being held to their reports. Experts are deposed.

- In New *York*, attorneys do not identify the name of the expert until the time of trial. The attorney may give broad details about the expert in a document that gives a summary of the expert's opinions. Law firm staff tries to find out the identity of the expert by taking clues and putting them into a software program. The expert is not deposed.

- In *Pennsylvania*, experts write reports but are not deposed.

Types of Reports

There are four primary types of documents prepared by liability experts: affidavits, plaintiff reports, defense reports, and supplemental reports.

Affidavits

In some states, experts are required to produce an affidavit (or certificate) of merit so that the attorney who is representing the patient can verify that somebody looked at this set of facts and believed that there was reason to pursue a claim.

I compare the filing of an affidavit of merit to a race. Imagine a group of horses are lined up at the starting gate in a race. In order for that race to start, there has to be an expert who is willing to sign an affidavit of merit. Then the attorney can file the claim and get more information and begin pursuing discovery, such as requesting an incident report and policies and procedures.

In some states the affidavit of merit has to be filed before a claim is started. In other states the plaintiff attorney has a certain period of time to supply the affidavit of merit after he or she has started the suit. Many conservative attorneys prefer, for their own peace of mind, to get an affidavit of merit before they file a suit. Others choose to start the suit because they're running out of time and get an affidavit of merit after the fact.

I've seen both patterns, and you may have as well if you're in a state that requires affidavits of merit. They're usually a simple, one-page document that says the expert has reason to believe there was a deviation from the standard of care and identifies who the expert thinks has deviated. It doesn't summarize any facts.

The affidavit is usually just a very simple form, a fill-in-the-blanks type of document. It is then signed, usually in front of a notary, and submitted to the attorney who has hired the expert. Be aware of when the affidavit needs to be completed.

In some states, the attorney talks with the expert about his or her conclusions, write the affidavit and supplies it to the adversary. The expert confirms the affidavit accurately states his or her opinion.

In New Jersey, for example, the attorney may file a complaint, which then must be answered by the defense. The affidavit must be given to the other side within 60 days after the defense has answered the complaint. Get specific information from the attorney involved. If the affidavit isn't filed in time, the plaintiff attorney may lose the right to proceed with the suit.

I was told about a case in which an expert was asked to provide an opinion on behalf of a plaintiff attorney and given a specific due date. Because the expert found that the nurses were not negligent, her opinion was that no basis existed for proceeding with the claim. However, she missed the deadline. Focusing on that point, the attorney refused to pay the bill.

A missed deadline can be more serious if the plaintiff's case is valid. The patient may sue the attorney for legal malpractice for failing to obtain an affidavit in time.

You, as an expert witness, NEVER want to be in the position of having the attorney blame you for not reviewing the case within the needed time frame.

Basis of Affidavit. Obviously, you'd like to base your affidavit on as much information as possible, including incident reports and hospital policies. However, the attorney might not be able to get more than the medical records until the suit is filed.

In signing an affidavit of merit, you simply assert a reasonable probability, based on the evidence available to you, that the care fell outside of acceptable professional standards. This initial position may be confirmed or refuted by additional information. You don't have to state with a reasonable degree of medical or nursing probability that there were deviations.

Ask the lawyer for a form and also get the caption for the affidavit (Wallace versus Empire Medical Center) from him or her. I recommend that you fax or email the affidavit to the attorney before signing it.

Once the attorney has approved it, sign the affidavit in front of a notary at a bank or courthouse. Bring proof of identification, such as a driver's license. Make a copy of the affidavit and mail the original with the raised seal to the attorney.

Other types of affidavits may be required. For example, I worked on a case in which a man fell face forward off his stretcher in the emergency room. He lost all of his teeth and had a head injury. There were no emergency room records in the medical record. The defense attorney insisted the chart was complete.

I convinced the plaintiff attorney that the chart was incomplete. I wrote an affidavit that was given to the judge. My affidavit said, "This man entered the emergency room at 12:00 p.m. The next bit of documentation is from 9:00 p.m. the same day. He was in the emergency room during that time frame. There have to be medical records for that time frame."

After the judge reviewed the affidavit, he ordered the hospital to produce the medical records that it asserted it did not have. The records were turned over.

Plaintiff Expert Reports

The plaintiff attorney requests his or her expert to prepare a report at the right time in the litigation. The timing may be based on the attorney's personal style or discovery end dates. Some plaintiff attorneys like reports written early in the suit before depositions are taken; others want them written after depositions and other document production (getting policies and procedures) is completed. The plaintiff reports set the tone for the suit.

The plaintiff expert may identify many deviations from the standard of care. The defense expert is going to rebut those deviations and identify the rationale for the opinion that there were no deviations from the standard of care.

Some deviations have no impact on the plaintiff. There may have been an error, but it had no relationship to the outcome. Particularly inexperienced experts tend to want to pile on as many deviations as they can, but this practice can work to their disadvantage.

The plaintiff expert's report that cites minor deviations gives the defense attorney an opportunity to attack the expert when he or she is being deposed. He or she may say "Well, you've identified this deviation. What is your theory about what happened to the patient as a result of it?" It may come out that the deviation had no impact on the patient.

Defense Expert Reports

The insurance companies in some areas ask for a preliminary review of a case when they have concerns their insured are going to be sued. The defense expert may be asked to review the case pre-suit.

After a suit is filed, the defense attorney and expert have the advantage of knowing the issues that the plaintiff attorney is focusing on. The defense expert has a much narrower job: to look at the issues that have been brought up by the plaintiff and to rebut them.

One of the things that happens behind the scenes is that sometimes the plaintiff expert's report is handed to the defense expert, who might agree with the plaintiff expert on some of those points that are identified as deviations. At that point, it's time for the defense expert to talk to the attorney and share concerns about whether this case is truly defensible and also to think about the deviations that the plaintiff expert has identified.

I'll give you an example of a report that I once reviewed that was written by a critical care nurse who was discussing deviations. She was hired by the defense to review a case, but she identified deviations from the standard of care in the report after she decided she couldn't defend it. Those deviations, however, were not germane to the issue. The issue was a reaction to a medication that was given in the critical care unit, but the expert wrote about minor and unrelated deviations.

The real issue alleged to have caused this person to die was the drug reaction. In talking to the expert, I realized that she had put in some things that were really not germane. She still couldn't defend the case, but in looking at her report, I pointed out to her that, while several of those deviations might have existed, they were not related to the outcome.

Supplemental Reports

Supplemental reports are written upon the request of the attorney when you receive new material, such as additional medical records or deposition transcripts. You have the opportunity to reaffirm, reiterate, or modify opinions based on that new information and also to rebut the opinions of the opposing expert in a respectful and a polite way.

Many experts, as a way of avoiding getting a last-minute request to review a batch of deposition transcripts and write a supplemental report, routinely ask attorneys, "Are there any more documents I need to review? Have any more depositions been taken?" An expert doesn't want to receive a lot of information at the last minute that has to be read, processed, analyzed, and integrated into the facts of the case.

Rebuttal Reports

An attorney may request a rebuttal report after the experts on the other side of the case have offered their opinions about it. If you, as an expert witness, are asked to write a rebuttal report, review the opinions that the other experts expressed and determine how to refute them.

In your rebuttal report, you don't have to reiterate the summary of medical events. Address the arguments and provide supporting evidence, standards of care, or deposition testimony to explain why you hold your opinions.

Components of Expert Reports

Contact Information

Put your full contact information at the top of the page. It can be in the form of a letterhead, or it can be typed in to create a letterhead. It should include a phone number and email address, as on a resume. It should also include your credentials. Sometimes experts don't think about putting their degrees after their name, and those are really important in terms of establishing some credibility.

Include a date. Write the report as a letter. Include the name of the attorney, law firm, and address. It helps to set the report apart by putting in bold the name of the plaintiff and the defendant. In some areas the case has been assigned a docket number or a case number, and the attorney wants to have that number included on the report.

List of Documents

The report always starts with a list of documents you have reviewed. These might include the medical records, depositions, answers to interrogatories, and, in some cases, expert reports. Everything that expert has been sent is part of the discovery of the lawsuit.

When you list medical records, clearly state the dates of admission. This list is invaluable when you are deposed because one of the inevitable questions is, "Have you reviewed anything else since you wrote your report?"

Summary of Medical Events

The next component is a summary of medical events, defining a very objective rendition of what transpired. The summary should have details focused on the issues at hand. You could spend pages and pages summarizing medical events, but the focus in an expert report is to look at what occurred and how that ties into the deviations—or the alleged deviations, if you're on the defense side.

The summary of medical events should be no more than about half of the report. Sometimes new experts spend too much time summarizing the care and not enough on explaining the standard of care.

Standard of Care

Next, define the standard of care. What would the reasonably prudent healthcare practitioner have done in the same or similar situation? The goal is always to compare the defendants to the reasonably prudent person and not to the expert clinician or the best clinician who ever walked the face of the earth.

The standard of care may include references to the nursing process, such as, "The standard of care requires the critical care nurse to perform an assessment, identify the appropriate nursing problems or needs, develop a plan of care, implement the plan of care, and then evaluate the response to the interventions." That's a nice blanket statement that can fit into many types of expert reports. If you are a plaintiff expert, what were the deviations from the standard of care? If you are a defense expert, how was the standard of care followed?

Then move on to the conclusions regarding whether that individual adhered to the standard of care or did not, again depending on whether you are working for the plaintiff or defendant. Some states require language such as "to a reasonable degree of nursing probability" or "to a reasonable degree of nursing certainty." The attorney in that venue will know what kind of mandatory language needs to be used.

Other state-specific language needs to be included.

The report needs to be signed. It is not considered valid without a signature in place. That's also the place to list your degrees if you have them.

Stylistic Aspects of the Expert Report

Use one consistent font and headers to divide up the material. Explain abbreviations and medical terms. Use short, clear sentences and the active voice. Describe the events in the past tense such as "The patient reached the floor at 1 p.m." instead of "The patient reaches the floor at 1 p.m."

Make the paragraphs smoothly transition from one to the other, and break up text into reasonable-length paragraphs. Be judicious with your use of bold, italics and underlining.

Be measured and conservative. There are some experts who personally attack the expert on the other side; that's bad form. Looking at this case not as a strong, passionate advocate but as an objective conveyor of a set of opinions regarding what has transpired.

Write your report to a layperson, clearly defining transitions from one point to the next, and also anticipating what the opposing expert's position is going to be.

Clearly define your opinions and then back them up with citations to standards or literature if you are sure there's nothing in that citation that's going to be used to contradict what you have written.

Only write the report when the attorney asks for it. There might be more discovery coming or depositions that are going to be undertaken. It's often premature to write a report at the beginning of the case.

The report should be well organized, and it should flow well and be neat in appearance. Use a proper format for reports.

Use block or indent style. This is block style.

∧∧∧∧∧∧∧∧∧∧∧∧∧∧∧∧∧∧∧∧∧∧

September 15, 2015

Mr. Thomas Sweeney, III, Esq.
Sweeney and Fisher LLC
1444 Highway 35 South
Ocean, New Jersey 07712

Re: Delores Kristian vs. Horizon Subacute Rehabilitation Center

Dear Mr. Sweeney:

As per your request, I have reviewed the provided following information as it relates to your client Delores Kristian and her stay at Horizon Subacute Rehabilitation Center.

∧∧∧∧∧∧∧∧∧∧∧∧∧∧∧∧∧∧∧∧∧∧

This is indent style.

∧∧∧∧∧∧∧∧∧∧∧∧∧∧∧∧∧∧∧∧∧∧∧

September 15, 2015

Mr. Thomas Sweeney, III, Esq.
Sweeney and Fisher LLC
1444 Highway 35 South
Ocean, New Jersey 07712

**Re: Delores Kristian vs. Horizon Subacute Rehabilitation
Center**

Dear Mr. Sweeney:
    As per your request, I have reviewed the provided follow-
ing information as it relates to your client Delores Kristian
and her stay at Horizon Subacute Rehabilitation Center.

∧∧∧∧∧∧∧∧∧∧∧∧∧∧∧∧∧∧∧∧∧∧∧

Federal Rules

The Rule 26 Disclosure governs the use of expert reports in
federal cases. This is a federal rule which guides production
of expert reports to provide opinion testimony.

It includes all of these very specific components for federal
cases. I have given you the rule below. Please note that Roman
numeral number "V" refers to a list of all of the cases in the
previous 4 years where the expert has testified *at trial or at
deposition*. This is a list of cases that you should keep for any
case because you may indeed be asked in a federal case to
provide this information. Note it only requires listing of cases

in which you have testified. You are required to keep a list for 4 years of all the cases in which you have been deposed or testified, including the name of the plaintiff and the name of the attorney, the county in which the testimony appeared, and the date. You don't have to identify whether it's for a plaintiff or if it's for a defendant. Eventually you will if you're testifying in federal cases. Sometimes in state cases the attorneys will ask for that information.

It's important for you to keep this data current in the event that you are asked for it. It will be very difficult for a busy expert to reconstruct this on the spur of the moment or upon request if it's not being kept current.

A busy expert will review lots of cases. Accurate records are essential.

∧∧∧∧∧∧∧∧∧∧∧∧∧∧∧∧∧∧∧∧∧∧∧∧

Rule 26

(B) Witnesses Who Must Provide a Written Report.

Unless otherwise stipulated or ordered by the court, this disclosure must be accompanied by a written report— prepared and signed by the witness—if the witness is one retained or specially employed to provide expert testimony in the case or one whose duties as the party's employee regularly involve giving expert testimony. The report must contain:

i. a complete statement of all opinions the witness will express and the basis and reasons for them;

ii.   facts or data considered by the witness in forming them;

iii.   any exhibits that will be used to summarize or support them;

iv.   the witness's qualifications, including a list of all publications authored in the previous 10 years;

v.   a list of all other cases in which, during the previous 4 years, the witness testified as an expert at trial or by deposition; and

vi.   a statement of the compensation to be paid for the study and testimony in the case.

∧∧∧∧∧∧∧∧∧∧∧∧∧

A federal rule provides protection from discovery of draft reports. Some states have had this rule prior to the passing of the federal rule, but the federal rule protects that work product aspect of the report until it is finalized.

It is:

> (B) Trial-Preparation Protection for Draft Reports or Disclosures. Rules 26(b)(3)(A) and (B) protect drafts of any report or disclosure required under Rule 26(a)(2), regardless of the form in which the draft is recorded.

I believe the thought behind this is to acknowledge that experts and attorneys have been sharing information and draft reports but not necessarily turning that over to the adversary.

It may be adopted by your state or it may not be, so that is important for you to know if you're working with experts or if you are an expert.

Why Keeping Records is Important

In the following situation, a woman suffered a stroke and arrested. The plaintiff contended the treating doctor should have done diagnostic testing when the woman was first disoriented and transferred her to ICU where she could have been more closely monitored.

The plaintiff's attorney had contacted the defense expert before the case was filed, two years before the defense had contacted him. The expert had not recorded the case and had forgotten his involvement in it.

After two hours of testimony at this expert's deposition, in which he testified there had been no breach in the standard of care, he was confronted with the handwritten notes he'd prepared for the plaintiff's attorney. In his report he'd asserted that the case had merit regarding liability and causation. Because he knew some of the physicians involved, he'd declined to go on record as a plaintiff expert.

The plaintiff's attorney had made the strategic decision to say nothing until the expert was deposed. He crafted deposition questions using report wording that he'd marked as an exhibit. The expert admitted to the authenticity of the signed report.

A $1.1 million settlement was reached in this Michigan case.

Proofreading

Proofreading is essential. It can save so much embarrassment at the time of a deposition or trial. It's crucial that you allow some time whether you're preparing expert reports or any other kind of document to proofread it. I am always amazed by the things that I *think* I have written versus what I have actually written. After I sit and prepare a report, I need to walk away and let it percolate and then go back in and review it. I make sure that I've picked up typos; I haven't left words out; I have my dates correct, and I have names of the plaintiff and the healthcare providers correct.

I have seen expert reports with incorrect dates, and wrong names of patients and defendants. Those are the kinds of things that you pick up on if you proofread carefully. It is essential to proofread any kind of report that you are working on, whether you're preparing expert reports, chronologies or timelines, Give it a little bit of time. Proofreading in paper form enables you to find errors that you might miss if you were looking at the computer screen.

Have a knowledgeable and trusted person look at your reports to identify anything that needs to be changed before it's submitted. This person should make sure that you haven't made any errors that your eye will just slide by. I think we all begin to lose some objectivity about what we've written, and our eye sees what we planned to write but not necessarily what's on the page.

Don't leave report writing to the last minute. It greatly increases the anxiety level of everybody, including the attorney who's sitting there waiting for the report to be delivered. You are likely to miss things.

Some people proofread start at the bottom of the page and read backwards, starting with the word that's at the bottom right hand corner and read in the opposite direction than your eye would normally flow, to catch words that have been spelled incorrectly. Personally, I don't use that method because it seems very awkward, but I see the value of looking at the document very carefully and making sure you allow enough time for the proofreading process to occur.

Always Keep Copies of Every Report

The following story will encourage you in this practice.

An expert prepared a report explaining why a particular nursing malpractice claim had no merit. She sent a copy to the attorney and stored the report on her hard drive and on an external drive. She didn't make a paper copy.

The attorney contacted the expert because he couldn't find a copy of the report. Unfortunately, her hard drive had crashed, and she couldn't initially find it until the next day. Had she not discovered it, the attorney might have expected her to again review the records and prepare a new report—most likely without being paid.

Don't risk this happening to you.

1. Use a cloud-based back up service that continually protects your files. Install a reputable antivirus program for your computer.

2. Always keep a paper copy of your report.

Beginner's Mistakes

Overview

Think of it this way: Your report provides the plaintiff or defense attorney with a set of directions that help to guide the plaintiff or defense attorney. If you wanted directions to a destination, you wouldn't want to hear about the roadside attractions or interesting sights off on side roads. You want simple and easy-to-follow directions.

Attorneys want to know how to get from here to there. They want a report that is easy to follow, grammatically correct, and succinct. They don't want to read about deviations from the standard of care that don't relate to the case. They don't want to wade through long-winded explanations. Most important, they will balk at paying for information that isn't directly relevant to their case, and they will think twice before requesting your services again.

You can enable a flow of repeat business by avoiding beginner's mistakes. You may shake your head in disbelief when you read some of these points. They have all happened to people I know.

Know the important legal issues to address. Don't get swept up in issues that have no bearing on the case. The nurse may not have written down the intake and output, but it had no impact on the outcome. Focusing on insignificant deviations is a beginner's mistake.

Know who the attorney represents. An expert wrote a report for the defense attorney, but she had been hired by the plaintiff attorney. She immediately put systems in place that have been strenuously reinforced ever since so that the expert is perfectly crystal clear which side she is on.

If you review the material and cannot assist the side who hired you, call the attorney and do not prepare a written report. Avoid the beginner's mistake of not talking to the attorney before writing anything.

Maybe the attorney doesn't want a report, because if the attorney gets the report, it may be necessary for him to turn over the report to the other side. That may vary depending on the venue where you're located. The important phone call to discuss the analysis of the liability should take place before anything is put in writing.

Provide sufficient information to substantiate your opinion. Don't offer a net opinion. A "net opinion" basically means, "Because I said so". Reports that rely on this give insufficient elaboration about the standard of care. For example, a net opinion defense report might spend the majority of the space summarizing the medical records, ending with a paragraph explaining the standard of care and then a statement that says, "I believe that the nurses adhered to the standard of care." This report would be attacked. The expert has to substantiate the opinion. It becomes a net opinion if it's not substantiated with specifics such as: "I find that the nurses documented turning and positioning. I find that the nurses notified the physician promptly at the early signs of skin breakdown. I find the nurses adhered to the standard of care when they consistently used the Braden scale in their analysis of the risk factors for skin breakdown. They provided the patient with a pressure-relieving mattress. They applied barrier cream to protect the skin from incontinence." Those specifics document adherence to the standard of care.

Don't put off writing the report until the last minute. Be clear on deadlines. Waiting until the last minute results in stress and the possibility that there will be mistakes in the report or in the analysis.

State "to a reasonable degree of nursing probability" or whatever term is needed in the state in which the case is located.

Be definitive in your opinions. It's not appropriate in the legal system to be wishy-washy. Take a position and then substantiate the opinion. Don't include words such as "it appears" or "apparently". These are terms that a generation of nurses were taught how to include in their charting — like "there appears to be red fluid coming through from the incision." In retrospect, it sounds ridiculous, and when it shows up in an expert's report, it can kill the report's credibility.

Anticipate the opposing expert's opinion. Think about the opposing lawyer and the opposing expert and rebut those perspectives. If you're on the plaintiff side, you should be thinking about how this case can be defended. On the defense side, you should be looking at what the plaintiff expert has addressed in order to rebut those opinions.

Avoid extreme words. Being extreme is using words like "horrendous", "atrocious" or "the worse nursing care I have ever seen in my entire life". Those types of extreme opinions make you sound, as the expert, like an advocate as opposed to being objective. It's the attorney's role to be a crusader and an advocate for his client. It's the expert's role to be objective and to explain the standard of care and whether it was met or was not met.

Don't bill for work that wasn't authorized by the attorney or client. If you have to do extensive research on the standard of care, that's not billable time; you should understand the standards. You can't bill the attorney for hours of time that aren't involved in the review of records or in the report preparation. That becomes a customer satisfaction issue and means you're at risk for not getting paid.

Stick to your area of expertise. Be firm in your convictions and do not let the attorney talk you into something you cannot support. Many states have become tighter in defining the qualifications of the experts by requiring "active clinical practice within 5 years" or "within 1 year". It will vary from state to state. Some states specify the expert cannot spend any more than 20% of his or her time doing non-clinical work, like expert work. Experts and attorneys should understand the restrictions. Some inexperienced malpractice attorneys might end up hiring somebody who doesn't fit the qualifications, but they pretty quickly learn not to do so when their adversary challenges them.

Use standards from the correct time frame. I proofread a report for one nursing expert who quoted 2014 standards in a case that occurred in 2009. That doesn't work. Standards have to relate to the time frame of the case.

Understand how your opinion fits in with the attorney's theory of the case. What does the attorney feel were the deviations? What were the deviations? Maybe the attorney doesn't know.

Don't overbill. Don't put in a tremendous number of hours on report preparation - more than can be rationally accepted by the attorney. Make sure that the report is not too long. I have seen some expert reports as long as 60 pages, with everything including the kitchen sink being identified as deviations.

Typical reports, on the long end, might be 6-7 pages, 10 pages maximum. These are ranges, but most reports do not exceed that length unless it's a very involved, very complicated case. The longer the report, the more ammunition the opposing attorney has to attack the expert's opinion.

It's important to be very focused and tailor the report to the issues in the case. Don't prepare a lengthy chronology unless you've checked in advance with the attorney, or the attorney understands you typically do this. Again, it may result in an invoice that's going to be larger than the attorney wants to pay, and it may not be indicated in that particular case. There is always a learning curve in doing expert work and taking on something new, and attorneys are not willing to pay for your learning curve.

CHAPTER 5

Learning Testifying Strategies

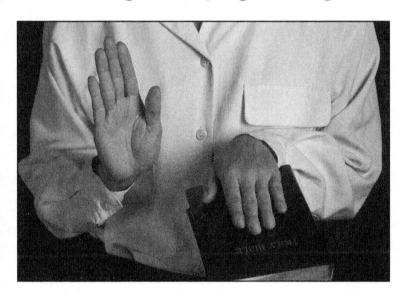

CHAPTER 5

Learning Testifying Strategies

Preparation

The key to doing well as an expert is rooted in preparation. You will need to have absolute mastery over:

- where information is located in the documents you reviewed

- facts

- identities of the defendants

- deposition testimony – yours and others'

- sequence of events

- your report

- your CV

- the opposing expert's report

- the names of the attorneys and who they represent

Your file should be carefully organized and indexed. Create a working system and stick to it. Use tabs, color coding, or whatever system works for you. As you gain experience, you'll learn what you need to have at your fingertips. Have your records as organized as possible. Organizing your file will help you stay calm and confident in the stress of a courtroom situation.

I saw an expert on the witness stand who did not have her records organized. The opposing counsel asked her to find a particular page in the nurses' notes. Her papers weren't in a binder, and she scattered them all over the witness stand. She couldn't find the document, and her composure turned into dust right on the stand. Don't let that happen to you. Be organized.

Rehearse how to give a concise explanation of your background. You should be familiar with your CV so that you can present your credentials. The stronger your opinions on the case, the more likely your CV and your clinical experience will be scrutinized. One of the things that new experts say is, "I just wasn't prepared for the attorney to spend three hours in my deposition asking me about my CV. The attorney asked about every professional thing I'd ever done."

Review your professional background and your CV as part of your preparation for testimony. Bring a few copies of your current CV to the deposition or trial. At a deposition, opposing counsel will want it. Expect to be asked about new items on your CV. At trial, your client will want a copy to use to go over your qualifications, and you'll need a copy in front of you.

Particularly if you're new at testifying, make sure you spend time with the attorney prior to your deposition or trial. Ask the attorney questions. He or she needs to understand what you're concerned about.

Make sure that you have all of the records and depositions. A lot of times, there'll be a long time period between when you've worked on a case and when your deposition or trial testimony is coming up. Make sure to ask your client if there are any new records, depositions, or anything else that hasn't been sent to you. Make sure you have it. You don't want to go into court trying to explain why you don't have all the materials.

Once early in my expert witness experience, the opposing counsel asked me in cross examination, "Did you review the deposition of the plaintiff?" I had to say, "No, I didn't know the deposition of the plaintiff had been taken." It makes you look like you weren't thorough in your preparation. You're responsible for asking the attorney if he or she didn't send you any relevant documents.

Know the strengths and weaknesses of your side and be prepared to handle the kinds of concessions you may need to make. Anticipate how to address the weaknesses of the case and answer the questions in a way that does not harm your client but allows you to be honest on the stand. Sometimes your clients want to focus on the strengths, but it's almost as important, if not more so, to understand the weaknesses and where you might need to do some explaining.

Keep the positions of the opposing expert in mind. Discuss the weaknesses of the case with your client. Attorneys should know the case weaknesses.

I always asked the attorney who hired me to tell me about the personality of the opposing counsel. This better prepares me to deal with the attorney's tactics.

Retainers and Fees

The fee that you charge depends on your location, your background, education, and experience. Fees will also vary depending on whether you received this case directly from the attorney or got it through a broker.

Attorneys expect that nurses won't charge the same rates as physicians.

Obtain a retainer from your client for the deposition and trial. Even if the state rules require opposing counsel to pay for your deposition, it is far more effective to hold your client accountable for paying your fees and then ask your client to collect reimbursement from the opposing counsel. It is sometimes difficult to convince insurance companies to provide retainers. If you must surrender your demand for a retainer from a defense firm, see if you can extract a promise of prompt payment.

Suppose your plaintiff attorney client challenges the prepayment and refuses to sign a deposition agreement. Don't schedule the deposition until you get the retainer and signed agreement.

I recommend a policy of required prepayment based on an estimated number of hours that it would take you to prepare and travel to a location to be deposed or to testify at trial. If you overestimated, refund the difference to the attorney at the conclusion of the trial. If you underestimate, invoice the law firm for the amount of time expended beyond your estimate.

Regarding an attorney who's challenging the prepayment and refuses to sign the deposition agreement, I would say that's something that has to be worked out with you and the attorney. But as the expert, you hold the cards. The attorney needs an expert to be able to support his or her case. If he's not willing to concede to your terms, and you've had a discussion and explained the rationale, you're still basically in the driver's seat.

I don't advise any expert to withdraw from a case without really seriously thinking about the issues and the consequences for the attorney and the case. It's far better to explain your policy as a professional, emphasizing that you can't proceed without receiving prepayment. Until you receive prepayment, you can't schedule a deposition.

Make sure all of your outstanding bills are paid before you go to a deposition or trial. If the plaintiff loses the trial, and you are the plaintiff expert, your attempts to collect a testifying fee are weakened by your loss of leverage.

Attire and Posture

Presentation is very important when you testify. Project a professional image. You can do this to some extent by your clothing and by how you carry yourself. Your dress should be professional, meaning a bit sophisticated. Women should not wear frilly clothing.

Make sure that your clothing is comfortable. You don't want to be so professional that you're actually stiff. Wear in non-constricting clothing. But there is a limit. I heard of a defendant nurse who came to the court room wearing scrubs. Another nurse came in wearing a purple pant suit. Neither is appropriate attire.

Dangling earrings may be distracting. Women should wear a limited amount of makeup. Its effects should be visible but not the makeup itself. Limit your jewelry.

Accidents can happen on the way to court. I know of an expert who slipped on ice across from the courthouse. She landed on her knee and ripped a huge hole in her stocking and lacerated her knee. The attorney bought a can of soda for her so she could put it on her knee to reduce the swelling. The experience did not help her composure. It was really not a good way for her to start her testimony experience.

I once took a bus to Manhattan to testify at a courthouse. I accidentally knocked off my earring when I shifted the bag I held containing my records and heels. I didn't realize until I got to the courthouse that I had also lost one of my heels. Fortunately, there was a store that sold both earrings and shoes, and I was able to replace what I lost and walk into the courthouse, perfectly groomed.

Videotaped testimony requires additional clothing restrictions. The video camera will actually add weight. Wear something dark in a solid color that is also slimming. Avoid patterned clothes because they can create moving lines when you shift position.

Sit up straight and look at the camera. The camera lens represents your jury. If you're being videotaped, you will usually be in a room with one or two attorneys, the court recorder, and the video recorder. It's very difficult to remember to look at the camera. Make sure that you address your answers to the camera and be animated.

Don't just stare at the camera. Make sure you're sitting still, not fidgeting, and not swiveling in your chair. Have your hands on the table in front of you or at your side in a comfortable position. Be sure to ask how the videotape is going to be used. The preparation is the same, but you want know if it's a videotaped deposition or if it's video to be used in the courtroom.

Experts have a tendency to put their hands in front of their mouths when they are testifying in front of a video camera. This reduces the comprehension of the people who are watching the tape.

Sometimes it's a good idea to be videotaped ahead of time for the practice. By seeing how you actually perform, you might pick up things you weren't aware of doing.

You may be deposed through video conferencing. One or more of the attorneys may be located in a separate area from where you are sitting. This is more cost effective than flying in an expert or a group of attorneys to a central location. Some depositions are taken over the phone. The advantage from the expert's perspective is not being distracted by the nonverbal body language of the attorney, who is instead a disembodied voice.

Testifying Techniques

The better you perform at a deposition, the less likely the case is to go to trial. The purpose of the deposition is to explore your opinions and to see what kind of witness you're going to make. You're being evaluated at depositions on more than the content of your report or your opinions.

In the deposition, answer the questions, but don't volunteer information. Give enough of an answer so that when you're questioned in an area later you can point to your deposition testimony and say, "Here it is."

Be aware of whom opposing attorneys represent. The opposing attorneys may recruit you to say favorable things about their clients. Be very aware when that happens.

You may be asked about something that is not familiar to you. Take the time to ask to see where that is in the record. This is perfectly allowable, and it's important that you ask. Don't ever assume that the attorney has it correct. If you want to, pause for a minute to consider all angles. When the attorney shows you the record that she is reading from, it may be important for you to look at a page or two before or a page or two subsequent to that note. You don't want to look at one fact in isolation; you need to remember the context of your case and consider that.

If you don't have something at your fingertips the attorney asks you for, you may say, "Excuse me, I don't have that right on the top of my head, but I can look for it" or "I can find it." This works if you know about where it is. It's important to know that record well and to have that file available to you so that you can look up information if you need to.

If I was asked where I found certain information, and I did not remember, I looked the attorney in the eye and said, "Would you like me to take the time to locate that in the record?" About 90% of the time the attorney said, "No, that's okay" and moved on to another question.

One of the techniques opposing counsel uses is to inaccurately rephrase or paraphrase what you have given as an answer to a question. It is your job as an expert to correct inaccurate rephrasing. When *you* rephrase the attorney's question, it shows you understand what the question is and know what you're about to answer. Listening is really the key.

Make sure that you understand the question and that you ask for clarification or rephrasing or repeating of the question so that you're clear on what is being asked. It's okay for you to rephrase by saying, "Are you asking me x, y and z?" Be very careful about multipart questions. The attorney may need to rephrase each part, or better yet, break the question down into pieces.

Attorneys will often ask you the same question rephrased in many different ways. This is the broken record approach. You can repeat your answer. Even though it's a slightly different question, if the intent of the question is the same, then your answer can be the same. Don't get caught up in having to give a convoluted or slightly different answer to a slightly different question that is really the same question. The attorney who hired you may begin to object when the opposing counsel keeps repeatedly asking the same question.

Here is what happened to me when I made a significant mistake in the courtroom. The defense attorney stomped into the courtroom, radiating nervous energy and anger. She dropped a copy of my *Nursing Malpractice* text onto her counsel table. When I looked at her, I knew that, as the plaintiff's nursing expert, I was in for a battle.

My client had asked me to testify on behalf of a man who was injured by an intramuscular injection in his buttock. The patient testified he felt an immediate pain that ran down his leg. There was nothing in the medical record that substantiated these symptoms. He developed a foot drop.

My direct examination went smoothly, and then I braced myself for the cross examination. In her short skirt and high heels, the defense attorney stalked over to the witness box and began her cross examination. She was quick in her questioning and eager to pounce. We sparred until she got to questions that went along these lines:

Attorney: "Did you see anything in the medical record that said the patient had pain down his leg?"

Me: "No."

Attorney: "The plaintiff testified he told his doctor about this. Would you expect the physician to document this, if this happened?"

Me: "I can't comment on what doctors are supposed to write or their standard of care."

Attorney: "Now come on, Nurse Iyer, you know what happens in hospitals and how medical records are put together. If the patient had told his doctor, would you expect to see the information in the medical record?"

Me: "I cannot comment on that."

Attorney: "Why didn't the physician put the information in the medical record?"

At this point, my client might have been objected to the continuing line of questions. I should have stuck to my guns and replied, "I do not know." Instead, I made a big misstep and answered, "Sometimes when there is a bad outcome, there is a cover up."

Oh, bad move! The judge, who had been mild up to this point, leaned over her area and breathed fire and smoke: "Nurse Iyer, you know better than to say that. You've been in my courtroom before."

She paused, and every eye in the courtroom was on me. I willed the floor to open up and deposit me one floor down. The defense attorney asked for a mistrial. The judge took a break, and then returned to the courtroom to tell the jury to disregard what I had said. "It is true that there are sometimes cover ups after bad outcomes, but we do not have evidence it occurred here." This remark made the defense attorney even angrier, and she asked for a mistrial again. The judge brushed the request aside.

My cross examination continued. The attorney took my *Nursing Malpractice* book off the table and opened it up to the preface. She said, "Isn't it true you wrote this book for plaintiff attorneys?" (She spat out the words "plaintiff attorneys.")

Since I have been trained to always request to see what the attorney is referring to when quoting my words, I took the book from her hands and said, "It says, "This book is written for plaintiff attorneys, defense attorneys, risk managers, and insurance claims adjusters." The defense attorney asked for a mistrial again because I used the word "insurance". The judge denied her request.

The defense attorney finished up her cross examination with my textbook by saying, "Isn't it true you wrote that the expert should present information to the jury to the lowest common denominator?" I believe the attorney thought the phrase would insult the jurors. I replied that the expert should explain things so the jury could understand her.

The attorney finally said the wonderful words, "That is all."

My client was gracious when I apologized for causing so much trouble. I learned some valuable lessons.

1. When asked the same question over and over, simply stick to the same answer.

2. Do not attempt to speculate as to why people did what they did. I should have simply said, "I don't know why the doctor did not chart the complaints."

3. You can't expect to anticipate how your words will be used. I never dreamt that the preface to that book could be twisted into something negative.

4.   The jurors were probably not offended by the "lowest common denominator." An acquaintance of mine who is an attorney said, "Pat, don't worry. The lowest common denominator on that juror did not know what the phrase meant."

I had a videoconferencing deposition in which I was retained to explain the pain and suffering that a woman experienced after she developed pressure sores. The attorneys who deposed me knew that my role was to explain what happened to this woman, and they knew I was not a liability expert. But the female attorney asked me about five different questions that all were geared to try and get me to give an opinion on liability.

I started saying to her, "Are you asking me my opinion about liability?" "No, we're not asking you that, you're not produced for that purpose", she responded. But then four other questions came in over the course of the deposition on my opinions, and I kept asking the same question over and over again until finally she stopped.

The attorney seemed unable to figure out my role. I was obviously not a liability expert, but she didn't really know how to ask me questions. Rephrasing can get you out of a lot of potential difficulties because you make it clear that you understand the question. You're also subtly directing the attorney by the way that you rephrase the question.

Trial Strategy

It's important to remember that you enter a new world when you become an expert. You don't necessarily understand the rules until you have an experience that makes you aware of them.

I went to a trial many years ago when I was a new expert. During the trial I sat on the bench next to another person who was waiting to testify; I whispered something her. The bailiff came and separated us and made me sit two rows back. He was trying to keep my voice away from the jurors, but I felt like a kid who had gotten caught talking in the classroom.

I learned from that experience that I had be mute and very careful to watch what I said, not make any comments in the bathroom when potentially jurors could be around, not make eye contact with them, or talk to them in the elevator or in the coffee area.

There are all kinds of rules. They are not immediately obvious if you're inexperienced, and I think that adds to the challenge of the experience.

Know who the other attorneys are in the room. Tell your client if you have worked for the opposing counsel in the court room. The attorney who hired you may be able to bring this out during your testimony. This will enhance your credibility with the jury.

In a trial you're speaking to the jury. You are teaching the jury, giving information, explaining the roles of healthcare professionals and medical concepts. The attorney gives you a lead, and you take that and run with it for the jury.

Speak clearly and distinctly. Use appropriate gestures, word images, and explanations to help the jury understand your opinions. Remember that the judge is in charge, and you must follow his or her rulings.

Face the jury because they're the ones you're speaking to, even though the question arises from the attorneys. Help them understand the important aspects of the case.

Cross Examination

Pay attention to opposing counsel's style. Some of the attorneys will be very friendly, almost inviting. Be careful about what you're disclosing. They can lead you astray.

The attorney isn't allowed to cut you off, so if one does, ask to be able to finish your answer. Sometimes the attorney attempts to interrupt you if the attorney you're working with is not paying attention.

Listen carefully to the questions, and see if you can anticipate where they are going. Be aware that the opposing counsel is trying to lead you into saying something helpful to his case. You need to be thinking, listening and planning while you answer questions.

Multitasking comes naturally to nurses. When we're working in a clinical area, we may be emptying a bed pan, but we're also checking for pressure ulcers. You use very similar skills in testifying. You're answering the question. You're paying attention to the words that are used, but you're also thinking what's behind that question. By listening carefully, you can detect misstatements. Sometimes the attorney calls the person by the wrong name. When you correct them, you present yourself as someone who is paying attention. They're not going to be able to intimidate you very easily. One attorney repeatedly called me "Dr. Iyer", even though both my attorney and I corrected him and told him I was not a physician.

Avoid getting defensive on the stand. Be factual, clear, and as confident as you can be.

In every case there tend to be discrepancies, some of them minor and some of them major. The best thing you can do is acknowledge them. There may be time discrepancies. Explain how you see them in terms of your investigation and your review of the record, but don't be upset by them. Don't get flustered; don't get defensive in any way. Simply admit there are discrepancies. The jury has to make sense of this.

It's important to know the difference between the facts of the case and the gray areas. Be very careful of making any assumptions or opinions. Sometimes the attorney may present something to you as fact when really it's the opinion of a physician or someone else, like another expert, on the case.

It's important to look for other data that supports your position. Suppose the attorney asks, "What do you think about this?" Give your opinion. That comes out of your preparation - individually and with the attorney.

Be careful of leading questions. The answer is usually "no" to leading questions like, "Isn't it true that" or "Wouldn't you agree?" You probably wouldn't agree with them. Careful listening will help you as an expert.

Multipart questions raise another red flag. Be very, very careful with those, and be sure to take each segment, analyze it separately before answering, and make sure that you can give an answer. It might be a question that in fact you cannot or should not answer. You can break the question into parts and answer each part separately.

Two other tactics that are opposite to each other involve the overly-friendly attornies who are trying to disarm you. They're very smooth and hypnotic. Try to avoid going along with them and answering every question with a "Yes, yes, I agree, yes."

The other side of that is the rapid-fire technique. Questions are coming at you one after another. The best strategy is to try to stay calm and again not get in that rhythm. Listen, take your time, think about your response, try to slow the pace and not get caught up in whatever the rhythm the opposing attorney is trying to get you into.

The angrier or the meaner the attorney, the better you're probably doing, and the sweeter and calmer you should be. If the attorney cannot attack you on the basis of your opinion, he or she will try the emotional tactic. It's important to understand some of the behaviors and don't take the attacks personally. Jurors tend to get angry with attorneys who attack respected expert witnesses. The attorney's tactics may backfire.

Hypothetical questions are designed to trip you up. The attorney typically changes some of the facts, although he or she includes enough facts that match the case to make the question confusing. The attorney hopes the jury will not see that it's hypothetical and will misinterpret it as part of the case. It's

important that you distinguish between a hypothetical statement or question and the facts in the case. You can do that by
first of all pausing before you answer. This is a great idea for
a number of reasons. First of all, it allows your client to step
in and save you if need be, to object and then tell you not to
answer for a certain reason. It also allows you to have some
time to think.

When you refer back to the hypothetical question, you may
want to start out by saying, "Those are not the facts in this
case." The opposing counsel typically tells you to answer the
question. But you've put it on the record that the hypothetical
example is just that. These are not the facts; this is not the
case at hand.

Many times the attorney will get very frustrated because he
is giving you that hypothetical example as a way to trip you
up. If you thwart him on that, he is going to become very
belligerent and frustrated sometimes, and he may keep it up.
You must answer a hypothetical question but be very clear
that it's a hypothetical example. You may also say, "I'm not
sure how to answer that, I've never had a situation like you
are describing."

You may be asked to answer a question as "yes" or "no." You
can say, "The answer depends," and the attorney may cut you
off and say, "No, it's a yes or no." Without getting argumenta-
tive, you simply need to state you cannot answer that question
with a simple yes or no.

The attorney is asking you that so that he can get something
on the record and avoid an explanation that may taint his case.
"Yes" or "No" do not correctly answer the question, and you

are sworn to answer correctly and truthfully. That's what you say.

Many times you can offer your explanation as to why it's not a yes or no answer. You can simply respond by saying, "Yes, sir (or "ma'am"), I will certainly answer a yes or no question when posed a question that can be answered with a yes or no." You need to exert some sort of control in this. You're not simply at his mercy. Keep that in mind.

I had an experience in which an attorney said to me in the court room, "I want you to answer this question yes or no" about a figure that I put together in a pain and suffering report that described the patient's weaknesses over the course of the admission.

As he asked me these questions, it was clear that he wanted to point out that I didn't put in all the examples of when the patient started feeling better. He kept wanting me to answer his questions "yes" or "no". I kept saying, "I can't answer that question; that was not the purpose of why I put together the information the way I did."

Finally, he threw up his hands and said, "All right, what was the purpose of the information?" This gave me the opening I needed to forge ahead. I gave my explanations. When he was done he took his notes, slammed them against the podium and stormed back to his seat. I had a brief thrill of victory.

Stay alert to the very end of your testimony. This may require effort if you're tired. You can see that it's winding down, and sometimes when your guard is down, the zinger questions come in. Stay at the top of your game until you're actually dismissed from the stand. The best words you can hear are, "You may step down."

CHAPTER 6

Answering Your Questions

Answering Your Questions

This section is designed to give you brief, easy-to-find answers to common and important questions related to your practice as an expert witness.

Reviewing Records

1. As I go through the records, I notice missing sections. Who helps me with that?

You don't need to directly contact the attorney. Call the attorney's secretary or paralegal and request what's missing.

2. Can I write on the records?

No. If you don't find you can help the attorney and are asked to send the records back, the copy you wrote on becomes unusable if the attorney decides to have another expert review the case. If you do take on the case, you could be asked in deposition about every mark you made on the records.

Use post it notes to flag key pages, and don't handwrite notes. These are discoverable, and, again, you may be asked about every note when you are deposed.

3. How do I get the incident report and facility's policies?

If you find merit in your preliminary review for a plaintiff attorney, tell the attorney what material you'd like. If you're on the plaintiff's side, you may not have access to either of these if the suit hasn't been filed. If you're on the defense side, ask the attorney if policies and the incident report can be provided to you.

4. What do I do after I review the records?

Call the attorney with your opinion about the case. If you have a favorable opinion, the attorney may want you to sign an affidavit of merit or write a report. Do NOT put anything in writing until the attorney asks you to do so.

5. What do I do with the records after I call the attorney with my opinion or write my affidavit or report?

KEEP THEM unless asked to either return them to the attorney or to dispose of them. If you can't support the opinion of the attorney who hired you, he or she may ask you to either shred the records or return them to the law firm. If you can support the position of the attorney who hired you, you'll keep the records until the case is resolved.

6. The attorney's office contacted me asking for dates for my deposition. What do I do now?

Offer to supply the law firm with 3 dates which are convenient for your deposition. Arrange to take the day off. The day before, confirm that the deposition will be taking place as planned.

7. Nothing has happened on the case for months. How do I find out what is going on?

Cases take an average of 4 years to resolve. Contact the law firm, ask to speak to the attorney's secretary, and inquire about it. Usually, a law firm doesn't notify the expert of a settlement. If the case has settled, and you haven't submitted your bill, you may not get paid. Bill promptly.

You can avoid difficulties by contacting the law firm every 6-9 months. If an attorney isn't getting back to you, investigate further. He or she may not be receiving messages or may have left the firm.

Withdrawal From a Case

Depending on when you do it, this may be a serious decision with far-reaching consequences.

1. What should I do if after I review the material sent to me, I believe I can't support the premises of the attorney who hired me?

You may decline to proceed further with the case. You might find that a case sent to you by a plaintiff attorney is defensible and that the nurses were not negligent. On the other hand, you might find that a defense case is indefensible. The sooner you decide, the more time the attorney has to find another expert if possible. Deciding that you are unable to help the attorney is not the same as withdrawal from a case. That is a far more serious and rare decision.

Once the expert has reviewed materials and has decided that she can support the side of the retaining counsel, and a report has been written, she very rarely withdraws from a case. By now, the expert has been named as being involved in the suit. The attorney may have no opportunity to bring in another expert.

2. Under what circumstances can I withdraw from a case as an expert?

The following circumstances are acceptable reasons for withdrawing:

    a. You develop a serious illness or die.

Be sure to have a system at home that records your active cases and that a family member knows how to use this system. Someone needs to inform the attorneys who hired you that you have a serious illness or died.

    b. New information dramatically changes your opinion about your previous position on the case.

This is rare but can happen. You must discuss your concerns with the attorney in this instance.

    c. You develop a conflict of interest, such as being hired by the defendant hospital to work for them.

For example, you may need to choose between being a plaintiff expert against a facility and taking on an assignment with that facility or one in its chain that places you in a conflict of interest.

    d. The attorney does not fulfill his obligations for paying invoices.

While this may be an acceptable reason, it is far preferable to do your very best to get paid. Use whatever strategic advantages you may have. If an attorney who hasn't paid outstanding bills calls to ask for something, say you'd love to provide it, but you need to be paid first.

The following reasons are not acceptable:

a. You decide that you no longer want to be an expert witness for this case because you don't like the role.

You may be working with an unpleasant retaining attorney or have disagreeable interactions with an opposing counsel at a deposition. You need to understand that it's nothing personal. The attorney is only doing his or her job. Your role may not be easy at times, and that's why not all nurses can fulfill the role of expert witness. Unfortunately, there is little room for error. The outcome of a case can rest on the skills of the expert. You can decide to stop accepting cases as an expert, but you are obligated to fulfill your responsibilities on any cases that are still active.

b. You move out of state.

When a deposition or trial is scheduled, arrangements will be made to bring you back from your new out-of-state home.

c. Your job responsibilities change.

Job responsibilities may make you less able to easily schedule depositions or trials. Advise your employer of your obligations as an expert if you are asked to accept a position that affects your availability. Employers are usually understanding if they know that you are legally obligated to see a case through to its completion.

3. What are the implications for a case if an expert withdraws?

The courts/judges are lenient if an expert dies or becomes permanently disabled or develops a conflict of interest. The attorney is usually permitted to find another expert and to get an extension of time. Should an expert withdraw from a case after a replacement can't be found, the retaining attorney may lose the case.

4. What are the financial implications for me if I withdraw as an expert?

A plaintiff attorney who is faced with the need to replace an expert may demand repayment of all money paid to you for your services. This is rare, but it has happened.

Depositions and Trials: A Checklist

Some of the material below is covered in the chapter on depositions and trials. I include it here (with some additional information) as a checklist to guide you through the key points of preparation for and participation in a deposition or trial.

1. How do I prepare for a deposition?

Go over the case materials carefully, referring to the post it notes you put on important documents and on deposition pages. (Do remove these notes before you arrive at the deposition or trial; otherwise, you'll have to explain every one to the opposing lawyer.) Thoroughly review both your report and that of the opposing expert (if you've received it). The latter opinion may suggest the kinds of questions the opposing lawyer may ask you.

Sometimes the attorney receives expert reports, depositions, and other medical records and forgets to send them on to you. Avoid having the opposing attorney present a document you should have seen but didn't by calling your client's office and asking for any new documents. Make sure that you have plenty of time to review these and to go over your report to see if the new information alters or reinforces your opinions. Bring a list of the new materials to the deposition.

2. What information in my possession is discoverable?

Anything the attorney sends to you could be discoverable, meaning the opposing counsel would have a right to see it. This includes the cover letter from the attorney (also called a transmittal letter), emails, reports, summaries of records, chronologies, summaries of deposition transcripts – in short, whatever the attorney sent to you.

3. Where will the deposition be held?

You can help to determine this. When the attorney contacts you for deposition dates, request that it be held at the attorney's office, a room in a courthouse, or a conference room in a hotel. Don't agree to have it in your home. Too many distractions abound. As for the specifics of the location, the attorney is responsible to organize those details.

4. What do I bring?

Basically bring whatever you received in the way of case materials. This includes medical records, depositions, answers to interrogatories, other expert reports, etc. Also bring your file, which should include any letters you received from the attorney and a copy of your report. Bring three copies of an up-to-date curriculum vitae. Before making copies, check it for accuracy.

5. What should I wear?

Wear dark, conservative, comfortable clothes. This attire is also appropriate for a trial.

6. What's the most appropriate conduct for a deposition?

Be relaxed yet alert. Always be polite. If you need a break, ask for one. Be sure to speak more slowly than usual. Spell out medical terms and people's names when necessary. This helps the court reporter.

7. The attorney sent me a copy of the transcript. What do I do with it?

Most states require that the expert review the deposition transcript within 30 days after receiving it. To miss the deadline means losing the chance to correct any errors.

If you find transcription errors, you create an errata letter. (Please note: this is not an opportunity to improve your answers.)

Here's a model for an errata letter.

Dear Ms. Attorney,

I have reviewed my deposition transcript and noted the following errors.

Page 14, line 8 states "I graduated with a B.S. in Nursing from the University of Massachusetts at Amrost." This should be Amherst.

Page 22, line 14 states "The nurse made a note that she'd restrained the patient." This should state "The nurse did not make a note that she'd restrained the patient."

By the way, the time you spend in review and in preparing the errata letter is billable.

8. I'm about to go to my first trial. How do I prepare?

See Item 1 regarding asking for new materials. This is equally necessary for a trial. Organize all materials in binders. If you'll be using public transportation, and the materials are excessively heavy, request to ship them to the attorney's office before the trial date so that he or she can bring them to the courtroom. Alternatively, ask if he or she can provide a copy of the medical record.

9. When does the attorney prep me for the trial?

Make your home and cell phone number available in case any last-minute discussions or preparations are necessary. The attorney may request that you come to the law firm for this. In my experience, it is more typical for the attorney to speak with the expert the night before the testimony is scheduled. The attorney updates the expert on what has transpired in the trial, shares any rulings the judge made that would affect the expert's testimony, and gives guidance on where and when to arrive at the courthouse.

Other preparations on your part include getting the name of the judge and parking recommendations. Ask if it's likely that the trial will be postponed.

10. I'm nervous about testifying.

Remember that you are the expert on the liability issues. Present your position to the jury with confidence and persuasion.

11. I didn't know jurors could ask questions.

Several states allow jurors to ask experts questions. Typically they write notes and hand them to the judge when your testimony is complete. The judge and attorneys decide which questions will be allowed, and the judge will ask you about them. These questions deserve the same degree of respect and attention as those asked by an attorney. Remember the jurors make the final decision.

12. What one word will guarantee a mistrial?

Never mention insurance. It may sound bizarre, but jurors aren't supposed to know that an insurance company is involved in defending a nurse, doctor, or hospital. The defense attorney wants to imply that the facility or healthcare provider would have to pay any award. This supposedly makes a jury hesitant to provide the award. Insurance companies are seen as having deep pockets.

Thus, if the defense attorney who hired you asks if his office has paid your bills, you say, "Yes." End of statement.

13. What other words might guarantee a mistrial?

Avoid saying anything the defense or plaintiff attorney tells you not to mention.

Here's an example. A medical malpractice case was based on a delay in diagnosis of lung cancer. A defense attorney claimed she'd told the defense physician expert witness not to refer to the plaintiff's history of smoking. (The judge had ruled the subject off limits.) However, at trial the physician mentioned the patient's smoking history and then said he didn't remember being told not to refer to smoking. The plaintiff attorney sought a judge to decide if the defense attorney and the defense expert should be sanctioned or found in contempt of court and pay attorney fees, costs and expenses incurred for the trial.

It's the attorney's job to tell you what the judge has ruled off limits. Your job is to listen carefully, remember, make a written note if necessary, and remain silent on prohibited subjects. You never want to be the reason for a mistrial request.

Reimbursable Expenses

1. Regarding deposition and trial work, what expenses are reimbursable?

The following expenses are generally considered reimbursable:

- Miles to and from a deposition paid at the current IRS rate

- Any form of express delivery used to send reports or records

- Cost of meals incurred while at a deposition or trial

- Parking fees at a deposition or site or airport

- Tolls going to and from a deposition or trial

- Transportation costs to get to a deposition or trial such a taxi or train

Save all receipts.

The following expenses are generally not considered reimbursable:

- Faxing costs

- Paper used to print reports or emails

- Telephone costs

- Gas

- Expenses for a family member, friend, or other person who may travel with you to a deposition or trial

2. What constitutes billable time?

Calculate billable time for activities that directly relate to the review of a case, preparation of a report, meeting with an attorney, or preparing to testify.

3. I have been notified that I have to fly out of state for a deposition. What travel costs and time are reimbursable?

The advice I provide is based on what I typically find experts charge for. Your client may have different procedures. Don't book your own flight or hotel. If the deposition is cancelled, you may not be reimbursed for those expenses. Provide information to the attorney's secretary or paralegal about your travel preferences and let the law firm do the booking.

Usually experts bill "portal to portal" This means you can bill for travel time from the time you leave your home to the point that you get to the hotel or deposition site. Some expert bill at half their hourly rate for travel while others bill at their full hourly rate. Any time you spend working with the attorney the night before the deposition or reviewing the file in preparation for the deposition is billable. Time spent eating meals, on personal hygiene, relaxing, shopping, or sleeping isn't billable. In summary, travel time to and from the site of the deposition, trial, or hotel and work on the file are billable. Personal time is not.

4. When are my meals billable time?

If you were working a 9 to 5 job, you wouldn't get paid for eating breakfast before work or dinner afterwards. The same goes for trial or deposition work. Breakfast and dinner aren't billable—with the following exception. If you have a long drive home from a deposition and stop for dinner, you can bill for that time.

Lunch is different. You can bill for a lunch eaten while you're waiting in the courthouse to testify. A lunch break during a deposition is billable time.

Lists You Need to Keep

1. Do I need to keep a list of cases?

Although you're not required to keep a list of cases you've reviewed, it's a useful practice.

- It provides a tally of how many cases you have reviewed on behalf of the plaintiff, and how many cases you have reviewed on behalf of the defense. Ideally, you want a good balance.

- It will also tell the number of times you have been deposed or testified at trial.

2. Do I have to keep a list of depositions and trials at which I testified?

Federal Rules of Evidence require this. Include the attorney's name, plaintiff's name, the county in which the case was filed, whether it was a deposition or trial, and the date. You must keep the information for 4 years.

3. Do I have to keep copies of reports?

Federal Rules of Evidence require experts to keep copies of reports for four years.

4. How long do I have to keep my file?

Business practices require you to keep your file on the case (but not the actual medical records) for 7 years after the case is completed. The file consists of copies of invoices and correspondence, as well as your written report.

5. When would a list of cases work against me?

If you testify in a deposition that you have such a list, the opposing counsel will probably request it. Then he or she might contact the attorneys who handled the cases and ask for copies of your reports. The purpose is to find your written opinions to similar cases to see if you ever took a contrary position.

6. What should I say in a deposition if I am asked if I keep a list of cases?

Don't volunteer this information. However, if the opposing attorney asks you about testifying, and you have a list, confirm this. Don't produce this list, though, unless the opposing attorney asks for it in writing. You always want to make him or her work for it.

Why do I need insurance?

Although it's very unpleasant to consider, you could be the target of a suit and need an attorney to represent you.

Here are some hypothetical worst-case scenarios:

1. Your report doesn't reach the attorney by the deadline, and the case is dismissed. The client sues the attorney for legal malpractice, and he blames you.

2. The attorney loses the case. His client claims that you, the expert, did not do a good job that caused the case to be lost.

Suits against expert witnesses are very rare, but an insurance policy can give you peace of mind.

Bringing Billing Records to a Deposition

The deposing attorney requested that I bring my billing records to a deposition. What should I do?
You're required to bring the billing sheets. These show the hours you put into the case.

Only provide information like invoices you sent to the client if asked and if the client agrees that you need to do so. If you're questioned about the billing sheets, adopt a neutral attitude. Experts get paid for their expertise. The deposing attorney isn't challenging your right to be paid. He or she wants to determine whether your review appears either inadequate or took up many more hours than warranted.

A few final words

By reading this book, you have discovered these key points:

The best way to get cases is to have great credentials and to do a great job for your clients. A professionally written CV or resume is critical for conveying your background and skills – the factors that make you an expert in your field. Create a strong first impression by carefully crafting a document that will wow a potential client. Well written and well proofread summaries of your experience will sell you as an expert, as I explained in Chapter 1.

There are many routes into becoming an expert. In Chapter 2, I shared how I got started as an expert and gave you tips you can use to increase your expert witness practice.

There are critical customer service, technical and professional skills associated with being an expert witness. Chapter 3 detailed the importance of great communication with the attorney and having a clear understanding of your role.

Experts need to meet a standard of excellence when crafting reports. Chapter 4 gave you pointers on preparing a well-organized and tightly argued expert report. Your wording in reports is critical and will follow you throughout the case.

Testifying is an experience that is often memorable, sometimes surprising and puts your communication skills to the test. What you say and do on the witness stand can make or break a case. Be well prepared and alert while testifying.

Lastly, ask questions, talk to your clients, meet their needs and be responsive. Becoming a successful expert witness takes time and develops over time. Be open to feedback; change and grow. Your confidence will soar with experience as you master this demanding role.

I work with expert witnesses and LNCs who want to get more clients, make more money and avoid expensive mistakes. When you are ready to make a financial and emotional commitment to growing your business, check out **LNCAcademyinc.com**. Let's work together to make your dreams come true.

Consider Writing a Review

Thank you for buying this book. When you enjoy a book, it is a natural desire to tell others about it. Amazon.com provides a way to share your thoughts and I invite you to write a book review. It is easy. Here are tips:

1. After going to the link below on Amazon.com, the first thing you are asked to do is to assign a number of stars to the book you think matches your opinion of the book.

2. Create a title for the review. This can be a simple phrase, like "Awesome guide." If you are not sure what to say, look at the titles of other book reviews.

3. It is easiest to write the book in a word processor and then paste it into Amazon.com. Your word processor will pick up typos before your review goes public.

4. Write the review as if you were talking to another person — you are — a person who comes to Amazon. com and is considering buying this book.

5. Include a description of what you found most helpful. Was it an idea, chapter, tip? Share that with the readers.

6. Next you may want to write who you think would most benefit from this book. Is it for beginners? Or is it more appropriate for someone with experience with this topic?

7. What if you have something negative to say about the book? You may always reach me at patiyer@legal-nursebusiness.com to suggest changes in the book.

8. If you include negative feedback in the review, keep a positive perspective rather than attack the author.

Here are some sample phrases:

- While overall the book was good, I would change it by. . .
- I don't think this book is right for. . .
- I would improve this book by. . .

Before you hit save, read everything over one more time.

Authors and readers appreciate book reviews and they get easier to write with time. Go to this link on Amazon.com to write your review. If for any reason it does not work, search for the book title + Iyer and it will show.

Link: **http://amzn.to/1MXJNQw**

Thank you,

Pat Iyer

Printed in Great Britain
by Amazon

37891989R00089